# The Tottenham Hotspur
## Football Book
## No. 3

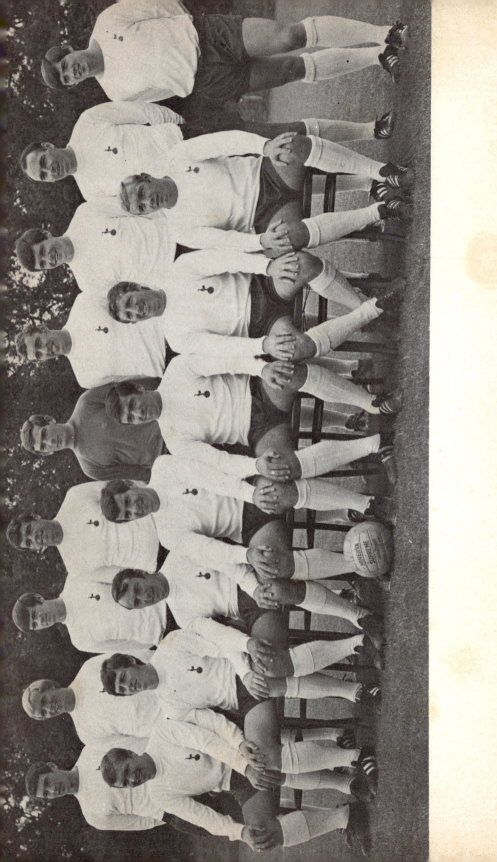

# THE
# TOTTENHAM HOTSPUR
# FOOTBALL BOOK

## No. 3

BY

## DENNIS SIGNY

FOREWORD BY JIMMY GREAVES

STANLEY PAUL
*London*

# STANLEY PAUL & CO LTD

*178–202 Great Portland Street, London W1*

*London, Melbourne, Sydney, Auckland*
*Bombay, Toronto, Johannesburg, New York*

*First published 1969*

09 097910 9

# Contents

| | Page |
|---|---|
| Foreword *by Jimmy Greaves* | 7 |
| Introduction | 9 |
| Spurs Supporters' Club | 15 |
| The Other Man Behind Tottenham | 27 |
| Working Hobby | 41 |
| Martin Chivers | 52 |
| Mike England | 64 |
| Joe Kinnear | 75 |
| Phil Beal | 84 |
| Jennings now Britain's best 'keeper | 93 |
| Roger Morgan—The Complete Professional | 106 |
| Jimmy for England | 116 |

# Foreword

*by*

## JIMMY GREAVES

*(of Spurs and England)*

As one of the older residents of White Hart Lane, I am delighted to be asked to write this foreword to the latest chronicle of a few of the achievements of a great club.

The 'Tottenham Hotspur Football Books', which have proved popular with all connected with the Spurs—players and supporters on the terraces alike—have helped give an insight to our day to day working and have spotlighted the personalities at the club.

I have been proud to be part of the Tottenham scene in the 1960s, surely the most glorious era in the history of the club, and would like to pay a personal tribute to the manager who signed me, Bill Nicholson. His dedication to Spurs has been a contributory factor to the success we have achieved—League Championship, Cup Final wins and a European Cup Winners' Cup victory—and his endless search for soccer perfection has enabled Spurs to establish themselves as a Top Team.

From the 'Glory, glory' days of the early 1960s, Spurs have built a new side, but Bill Nicholson has rarely deviated from his course of providing entertainment as well as results. This cannot have been an easy line to take in an era of tactics and massed defences.

Spurs have provided their loyal supporters with great players and some exciting moments, always with the emphasis on good football and attacking play. We welcome these Tottenham books as a record of our endeavours and those of our predecessors.

Push and run, the style adopted so magnificently by Arthur

Rowe's team of the 1950s, was succeeded by Super Spurs and the 'Glory, glory' days. And I can assure all Tottenham supporters that even when the results have been disappointing the aim at White Hart Lane has been the same—second best is not good enough.

Lastly, a word about Dennis Signy, the author of the Tottenham Football Books. I have known him a long time, from my early days at Chelsea, and he has been on the scene during my England career and my years at Tottenham surveying the soccer scene and reporting on events and stories. He has seen many landmarks in my career and I hope he will be around to record a few more.

Good luck to this latest Tottenham book! I hope it gives as much pleasure to readers as its predecessors—and that we at White Hart Lane can go on providing material for further editions.

# Introduction

The yellowing newspaper cutting from May 1967, looks mockingly from my desk as I write. The headline on the sports page following the Spurs success against Chelsea in the F.A. Cup Final has a hollow ring.

'Spurs' target to take over as the new Real Madrid' wrote the exultant headline writer over a story proclaiming Tottenham's return to Europe and manager Bill Nicholson's bold statement: 'Tottenham Hotspur are nothing unless they are competing in Europe.'

May 1967—only two years ago. But a lifetime in soccer. Spurs, I am afraid, have become victims of their own magnificent success in the 1960s and the fans have come to accept manager Nicholson's defiant words: 'Spurs have got to be the best in the land. Not the second best.'

Season 1968–69 will go down as a year of disappointment for the devotees of soccer at White Hart Lane although, in all, the team made a bold bid against odds to stay with the elite of the First Division and did commendably well.

Sixth in the championship race. Semi-finalists in the Football League Cup. And they reached the sixth round of the F.A. Cup. Not bad. Unfortunately, not good enough by the exceptional standards set by the super-Spurs of recent memory and the demands of manager Nicholson.

The snag was that Tottenham set their sights too high and the disappointment, shared equally by players and supporters, came when they fell below their own Everest-high standards.

Without wishing to be labelled a propagandist or seeker after excuses, I would submit that Spurs hauled themselves to sixth in the First Division table despite the lengthy absence of Martin Chivers, who was just hitting peak form when he was injured, the loss of Joe Kinnear and the recurring ankle trouble that kept Mike England below his top form for long periods.

Then there was the problem caused by the departure of Dave Mackay . . . Bill Nicholson, ever a realist, faced up to his problems at White Hart Lane when Cup defeat at Manchester City last March meant the club facing a quarter of a season apparently without object.

'The main thing is we haven't replaced Mackay yet,' he announced.

How do you replace Mackay? Or a Danny Blanchflower? Or a John White? You seek a fresh face, a new look or a new blend—but it is hard to replace a star of the first magnitude.

In recent years Spurs have had the success. It all revolved around the team. With characteristic honesty Bill Nicholson said last season: 'At present we haven't got the team. The club can be held responsible. That means the manager is responsible. 'EVEN SO YOU CANNOT EXPECT TO BE ALWAYS ON TOP.'

Clubs have to be successful or their supporters want to know why not. Bill Nicholson, more than most managers, appreciates this simple fact of soccer life. For him the problem is made more acute by the success he has given Tottenham.

Liverpool have been on the crest of a wave for five seasons with more or less the same players. The time will come when they have to replace four or five players at the same time. Then they will experience what Spurs have been trying to recover from.

Spurs have been in the process of rebuilding for fresh glories since the double side broke up. The 1967 Cup Final success was an unexpected bonus—unfortunately it accentuated the problem.

The cries went up last season for Bill Nicholson to buy. It is easy for success-saturated fans to say Spurs should buy this player or that player; they don't know the problems the manager of a top club faces.

In the course of a soccer season I watch some 150 Football League matches. I'd certainly like a fiver for each time I saw Bill Nicholson, Eddie Baily or one of the Spurs scouting team at the matches I selected.

Bill Nicholson has spent hundreds of thousands of pounds to bring glamour, personality, skill, strength and, by no means least, goals to White Hart Lane. Why doesn't he rush into the transfer market to plug any gaps in the side?

Spurs, after all, are among the wealthiest clubs in the land. They made their biggest-ever profit in season 1967–68, despite the signing of Martin Chivers. After handing over £33,808 in corporation tax, they were left with a profit of £79,790.

This was the best year Spurs had had since the 1962–63 season when they were in Europe for the first time and made a gigantic £131,820—reduced by income tax to a net £68,926.

Roger Morgan arrived at White Hart Lane last season for a five-figure fee, but the anticipated spending spree did not become a reality. Let Bill Nicholson explain. He says: 'If you get the player you want it is not a gamble. These days it is not easy to buy and it is becoming more and more difficult for clubs at the top. Because of the advancement of football, players are over-valued today. Transfer fees have risen out of all proportion.

'Supply and demand has led to this situation. Players are the real assets of a club today—money is an embarrassment.'

Spurs do not move for a player until he is available. The search for fresh talent goes on week in, week out but, in soccer that is, money is no guarantee for success.

So, was the 1967 headline of Spurs emerging as the new Real Madrid a mere pipe dream? I would hesitate to write them off at any time because Tottenham, by nature, are a top club and manager Nicholson is a perfectionist who commands respect and generally gets success.

His record as a manager is remarkable. The more remarkable because he scorns the shelter of a contract. Elsewhere in this book Tottenham chairman, Mr. Fred Wale, reveals that money has not been discussed between manager and the Board since Bill Nicholson was offered the job in season 1958–59.

Bill Nicholson has served Tottenham well since the day in March 1936, that he presented himself at White Hart Lane as a 16-year-old acquisition to the ground-staff. Thirty-three years later this forthright Yorkshireman who works, eats and sleeps Tottenham is still there.

Spurs finished eighteenth in his first season, but since then they have never finished lower than eighth. They have won the League, the Cup three times and the European Cup Winners' Cup. Under Nicholson's guidance, Spurs have been one of the few clubs whose riches have enabled them to reject most of the negative patterns of the modern game.

During his time he has seen one team destroyed by age, injury and death. Patiently he built another . . . and the search for the best still goes on.

If players, as Bill Nicholson says, are a club's assets Spurs have a fine start in their fresh bid to combat the current success sides. I doubt if there is a finer goalkeeper in Britain than Pat Jennings. Mike England still lays claim to the tag of No. One centre-half in the home countries. And Jimmy Greaves . . . he's a law unto himself. Suffice to say that he was the top scorer in the First Division last season.

Alan Mullery is currently England's first choice right-half and there cannot be a more honest and industrious player in the game today than Tottenham's popular skipper. Alan Gilzean is a regular choice for Scotland . . . Cyril Knowles is an England international.

As Bill Nicholson says: 'The crowd at Tottenham has come to expect star players in the team. If they see good players supplying attractive football they'll continue to turn up, whether we are winning competitions or not. Everybody likes to win, of course, but it's not everything. We will still get support if we play the right sort of football.'

A waiting list for season tickets is evidence of that. There are obviously a few hundreds, at least, who pin their faith in the ability of master manager Nicholson to guide Spurs to fresh triumphs.

He is a hard taskmaster. As he put it to me: 'If you don't win anything, you have had a bad season.' Sixth in the table does not satisfy Bill Nicholson. He regards a lack of success as a reflection on everyone in the club, from manager to players to coaching staff to the scouting system. 'A club of Tottenham's standing should get into Europe,' he argues.

The Nicholson aim is the Football League championship. He says he is old-fashioned enough to feel that a team must win the championship of the best competition in the world to prove anything.

Dave Mackay described Bill Nicholson to me as 'an inspiration'. That's why it is not so silly to look back at that 1967 cutting and read that Spurs hope to take over the Real Madrid mantle.

One phrase sums up Bill Nicholson's outlook. When we discussed the question of his lack of contract, he answered: 'What is the use of a contract. YOUR ONLY SECURITY IS YOUR ABILITY.'

Spurs march forward in search of more success, more Glory, Glory, led by a man whose ability is proven by the record books.

The League championship is the aim. Europe is the yardstick. Bill Nicholson aims high. Alan Mullery describes him as 'a footballer's manager.'

There will be more than footballers cheering and wanting to slap Bill Nicholson on the back when Spurs go marching on to fresh triumphs.

Long-serving Spurs defender Ron Henry performs the opening
ceremony at Warmington House. On the left: Tottenham director
Mr. C. Cox. On Henry's right: Supporters' Club President,
Mr. John Agram, J.P. and the Mayor of Haringey.

# Spurs Supporters' Club

The story is told of the occasion when Danny Blanchflower decided it was time his son, Richard, took an interest in football. So the irrepressible Danny bought the boy a season ticket for White Hart Lane.

Danny, skipper of the Spurs side of the fabulous 'Glory, glory' era, was keen to check how the youngster fancied watching Dad at work among the other great players of the double-winning side.

'What's your favourite team?' young Richard was asked.

And back came the surprising reply: 'Tranmere'.

Why Tranmere? The significance of the reply has never been explained to me, but the moral of the story is in the fascination of what goes to make a football supporter.

When I was a boy I supported Grimsby from afar—chiefly because I had read that the club was hospitable and gave gifts of fish to visiting teams. I never went to Grimsby until I was in my 30s.

Sheffield United also took the fancy of young Signy—there was an irresistible appeal about the nickname 'The Blades' and I envisaged eleven he-men with steely qualities. My enthusiasm was heightened when United reached the 1936 Cup Final and I willed them, albeit unsuccessfully, to beat Arsenal.

Red and white striped shirts had a particular appeal to me at the time and when the time came for me to venture forth physically to support a football team I got out a bus map of London and worked out, with the aid of a ruler, the team nearest to my home in N.W. London.

The sight of Warmington House to let opened a new era for the
Supporters Club.

Brentford (the club I was later to manage) edged a victory over Arsenal and Q.P.R. and, on my first visit to Griffin Park, my delight knew no bounds when I found my new heroes sported red and white striped shirts.

The object of this personal reminiscence is to point out the indefinable in a man's attachment to a football team. I still ponder how Brentford claimed my affections—Griffin Park is ten miles from my home and it is far easier for me to get to Q.P.R., Arsenal or Spurs. Mind you, there was no question of my ever supporting Arsenal. You loved 'em or you hated 'em in those days—and too many of my school chums supported them for me to toe the line.

Perhaps the ruler slipped! I don't know. I do know that I grew up as Brentford-minded as any man and proudly told people that I supported the team of the county town of Middlesex.

All of which leads to my main point: what makes a Tottenham supporter tick? Is there an average Spurs supporter?

John Harris, 55-year-old bachelor secretary of Spurs Supporters' Club, supplied me with many answers to my questions and as we sat in his office at Warmington House overlooking the front entrance and forecourt of the Tottenham club I drew an interesting picture.

Spurs Supporters' Club was 21 years old (or should I say 'young'?) last August—but Mr. Harris revealed the startling statistic that of a record membership exceeding 7,000 the minority came from the immediate Tottenham or Edmonton areas.

In the files at Warmington House, a few paces along the High Road in Tottenham from the Spurs ground, there is evidence of the diversity of support for the team known as the Lilywhites by generation after generation.

Families have moved from the Tottenham or Edmonton districts, but they still pour in to White Hart Lane on match days from their new homes in the North London suburbs or in Hertfordshire and other Home Counties.

Spurs, it may surprise a few of you to know, have strong support in the North of England. And there is a Tottenham pocket of resistance in East Anglia.

A Spurs-mad group of some 50 people—the description is given by Mr. Harris—drives to Town through all sorts of weathers to support their favourites. At the end of each season they meet to discuss what pleasure (or otherwise) following Tottenham has given them and to analyse the future. John Harris travelled to join them for their last end-of-term rally.

17

Spurs captain Alan Mullery receives the Supporters' Club Player of the Year trophy from his former Fulham and England colleague, George Cohen (*left*).

What has Stockport, Cheshire, in common with Tottenham, N.17? I don't know, but Spurs Supporters' Club has an active group in the Stockport area.

Last summer a group of Britons working overseas in the heat of an oilfield in the Middle East got together and wrote to Mr. Harris asking if they could form a group in that remote outpost of soccer fanaticism.

Spurs have active supporters in Sheerness and a good following in The Netherlands. Maybe that is an 'aftermath of the club's triumph in the European Cup Winners' Cup competition earlier in the 1960s, a game the B.B.C. chose to feature in their 'Match of the Decade' series last close season.

For six months last season a letter arrived at Warmington House from Holland once every four weeks containing a postal order for £1. With the sixth pound came the polite enquiry: 'Can I be a

18

A kiss for Player of the Year Mullery from Mrs. Pat Bush.

Life Member of Spurs Supporters' Club—you've got the other £5!'

Spurs have what Mr. Harris describes as a 'terrific following' in Ireland. This grew in the Danny Blanchflower era, and has stayed intact with the arrival of Northern Ireland international goalkeeper Pat Jennings.

'They're Pat Jennings crazy now,' says John Harris.

Spurs have support in Scotland—one youngster travels south to all big matches—and perhaps this was built up by the late John White and Dave Mackay.

In the days of Ron Burgess, Terry Medwin and the Jones's, Spurs had a Welsh following—not so strong these days.

There is a branch of the Spurs Supporters' Club in Malta, all fanatical followers who enjoy keen rivalry with the supporters of other big teams living on the George Cross island.

John Harris, who grew up as a supporter of Clapton Orient, graduated to White Hart Lane after a brother-in-law introduced him to Spurs years ago. His reason for switching allegiance is simple logic: 'Tottenham played better football than Orient.'

Not all supporters are as faithful and loyal as the likes of dozens I could mention. Many girl football followers—I disdain to use the word 'supporter'—switch allegiance when their favourite player leaves a club. Johnny Brooks took a few with him when he went to Chelsea—but Spurs gained on the deal when they signed Jimmy Greaves . . . and a good few Chelsea admirers of the talented marksman, too.

'We don't encourage fan clubs,' says John Harris. 'We support a team and not an individual. Our Player of the Year award gives social interest, but it is not a deviation from our policy of overall support.'

Player-supporter links, of necessity, have diminished. In years gone by—before the dreaded box glued people in front of a television screen—players such as Ron Burgess and Eddie Baily lived in the roads adjoining the Tottenham ground and were more available to attend functions. Today the players are spread further afield . . . in Surrey, Essex and Hertfordshire.

How did Spurs Supporters' Club come into being? It stems from a group who met at Stamford Hill back in 1948 and organised away trips to watch the team. They decided to form a committee and, when Spurs drew Arsenal away in a Cup tie, the chairman of the club at the time, Mr. Fred Bearman, said they could purchase tickets as a body.

Pat Bush, the Spurs Supporters Club Queen who went on to win the national title at Torquay, has a celebration glass of champagne. *On the left:* John Harris, the Supporters' Club secretary and Ted Marshall, the chairman. *On the right:* John Agram, J.P., the club president, and Harry Goss, social officer.

'They appreciated the facility, just as we today equally appreciate the help that Tottenham Hotspur gives us,' says Mr. Harris.

The first meeting of Spurs Supporters' Club was in a church hall. Some of the founder members are still around. There are no greater supporters of Tottenham Hotspur than two of them, Mrs. Fuller and Mrs. Patten, affectionately known as 'Gert and Daisy' for two decades. Both ladies, now in their 70s, retain interest and stand in the enclosure to support their favourite team.

The Supporters' Club led what John Harris describes as a 'hand to mouth' esxitence. They needed every scrap of voluntary help they could get. Back in the late 1940s the club would buy a dozen rosettes and a dozen balloons for sale on match days—and increase the numbers to two dozen for the next home match if they sold out.

A section of the 1,000 supporters air-lifted to Rotterdam to cheer
Spurs when they reached the final of the European Cup Winners' Cup.

Things improved when the church opposite the Tottenham
ground allowed the Supporters' Club the use of a club house—
Arthur Rowe, the Spurs manager of the time, opened the premises
—but the hall was later demolished to make way for prefabs and
the Supporters' Club moved on to new headquarters at a nearby
tavern and later a restaurant.

The turning point came when a life vice-president of the
Supporters' Club saw that 744 High Road, Tottenham, was
empty . . . and Warmington House became the new home of the
club. A lease was signed and renovations took place. Inside three
years membership of the club had trebled. Eddie Jones became
the secretary, to be succeeded by John Harris.

Mr. Harris, longest serving continuous member of the committee, is a fund raiser and link between supporters and their club.

Each year the Supporters' Club build up a new membership,
although they try to retain numbers if possible. 'Gert and Daisy'

Thousands of supporters . . . the day after Spurs won the cup in 1967.

still have their 1948 membership numbers. There are over 100 Life Members, active vice-presidents and a host of voluntary helpers.

The Supporters' Club holds four functions each year: the Player of the Year award dance (members vote in the close season), the Queen competition, an annual dinner-dance and an end-of-season dance. Mrs. Pat Bush, Spurs Supporters' Club Queen last year, went on to win the national title and to appear in television advertising.

What are the benefits of being a Supporter of Spurs? Note the capital 'S'. First and foremost, of course, is the use of Warmington House, with its lounge, bar and refreshment facilities. A good place to wait out of the rain.

'The club house is for service to members,' says John Harris. Younger members can watch television in their lounge—Warmington House is a good social centre.'

The sorry scene for supporters who had not heard the news—the match against Q.P.R. postponed.

In the event of an all-ticket match, or an away match, Spurs Supporters' Club can virtually guarantee their members a ticket, which can save hours of queueing. Cheap travel to away games is arranged, and the club can charter trains and bring the rail fare down by half.

Most clubs recognise the work of their Supporters' Club by making an allocation of Cup Final tickets—in the knowledge that they go to the genuine supporters of the club.

When Spurs played their Cup Winners' Cup Final in Holland an air lift of over 1,000 supporters was organised.

Spurs Supporters' Club have their pet hates in soccer watching and, as a body, are anti-hooligan. Some of the antics of a minority section at the Park Lane end of the Tottenham crowd are abhorred, and the throwing of toilet rolls is discouraged.

'Hooliganism in soccer? In the Supporters' Club we don't know of it,' says secretary Harris. 'Acts of hooliganism are committed by a group of teenagers who wear the scarf of a particular club for an occasion—sometimes it is Spurs.

'If you went to Euston Station most Saturdays you would see these hooligans finding the cheapest excursion of the day and then sending a youngster of 12 or 13 to buy a few half-price tickets. Then these louts would travel off to a match.'

Spurs Supporters' Club got together with British Railways to combat this problem and the decision to charter coaches on trains (or the whole train) was taken as an alternative to half-price tickets. Spurs Supporters have had no bother on their travels.

The ratio of support is five adults to one junior in the membership of Spurs Supporters' Club and John Harris says: 'Vandalism in soccer is in the minority, stemming from the days of Mods and Rockers at the seaside.'

John Harris's mother, now aged 85, is one of the oldest of Spurs travelling supporters; at the other end of the scale are the day-old children of members who are enrolled at birth. There is a keen family interest in the Supporters' Club, husband and wife and children travelling together to matches.

The success of Spurs affects the Supporters' Club. Sales are reflected by the attendances at White Hart Lane. But John Harris is always active answering queries and sending autograph sheets.

Ted Ditchburn used to be a liaison officer between players and supporters, but the position has not been maintained into the 1960s.

One of the features of the 'Glory, glory' days of the early 1960s was the enthusiasm engendered by the Tottenham 'Angels', but John Harris says: 'The average Tottenham supporter is not vocal enough at home games.'

Members of the Supporters' Club, like the rest of us, moan at the team when things aren't going as well as they should. 'Drop the lot' . . . 'bring the youngsters in' . . . 'why not play so-and-so'. The phrases can be heard on the way home from most away trips.

A Spurs Supporter (even with the capital 'S') is as human as the next man. But . . . he'll react to McNamara's Band or 'Glory, glory, Hallelujah'. He won't hear a word against his favourites from a rival fan. He can be vocal to the point of erudition in discussing the respective merits of Jimmy Greaves and Roger Hunt.

He's a genuine supporter who has committed his loyalties by paying his subscription. He may not be vocal enough at White Hart Lane for John Harris . . . but he can make himself heard.

Spurs Supporters come in all shapes and sizes and age groups.

They flourish in Holland and the oilfields of the Middle East
Some live in Stockport, others in Scotland.

How each one became a supporter is an individual story.
Today they are linked by the common bond—they think their
team is the greatest. Call them Lilywhites or Tottenham or Spurs
. . . it's the same.

Take a look at this 1950 lyric to McNamara's Band. The names
have changed, but the sentiments the same:

'We are the Spurs Supporters, and we love to watch them play.
We go to all the home games, we go to those away.
With us supporters following them we know they must do right,
We loudly cheer when they appear, the lads in blue and white.

'We're very proud of our football ground, it's known throughout
    the land,
And whilst we wait for the game to start we listen to the band.
And when we see the teams come out you should hear the roar,
We know it won't be long before the Spurs they start to score.

'The Ref his whistle proudly blows, the linesmen wave their
    flags,
The 'Duke' is ready to kick off whilst hitching up his bags,
We cheer old Sonny Walters as he toddles down the line,
And the ball like magic is in the net and makes us all feel fine.

'There's Ronnie Burgess with his skill, holding up the line,
With Nobby, Bill, Alf and Charles, way up there behind,
And not forgetting good old Ted whose hands are sure and
    strong,
And Eddie and the Leslies who are always up along.

'And when the game is over, when the game is through,
We cheer the winners off the field and the gallant losers too.
The Cockerel proudly wags his tail (he gave the Spurs their
    name),
In honour of the Lilywhites who always play the game.

'Now come on you supporters and join our merry band.
No matter what your age is, we'll take you by the hand.
We'll pin a Cockerel on your chest, it shows the world that we
Are members of that loyal club known as the S.S.C.'

How could anyone support Tranmere in face of that?

26

# The Other Man Behind Tottenham

As a player in the Spurs' push-and-run championship winning side of 1950–51 he was 'irreplaceable'. Arthur Rowe, his manager at the time, said so.

He would get a majority vote for an inside-forward berth in any nominations for a best-ever Tottenham side of the 74 years since the club embraced professionalism—yet Eddie Baily might well have become a Chelsea player because Spurs forgot him.

Today Baily, at 43, is assistant to manager Bill Nicholson, his playing colleague from the push-and-run side, at White Hart Lane, and has built a reputation as a coach. He is trying to put into practice what he learned as a player: 'Do the simple things quickly and pass a ball accurately.'

Clapton-born Eddie, the youngest of five sons and two daughters, built a national reputation as one of the greatest inside-forwards of the post-war era and as a typical Cockney character. He was a 'Cheeky Chappie' and it reflected in his play.

His late father was an all-round sportsman and the Baily boys all achieved a good standard of amateur football or of cricket. Eddie's brother, Len, it was reckoned, might have made the grade as a pro. player.

Eddie played inside-forward for Detmold Road Junior School (now Southwold) and later at Mount Pleasant Senior Boys' School. 'I can't remember playing anywhere else from the age of ten,' he says.

He was chosen for the same Hackney district schoolboy side as Alf Noble, who later played for Leytonstone and England amateurs,

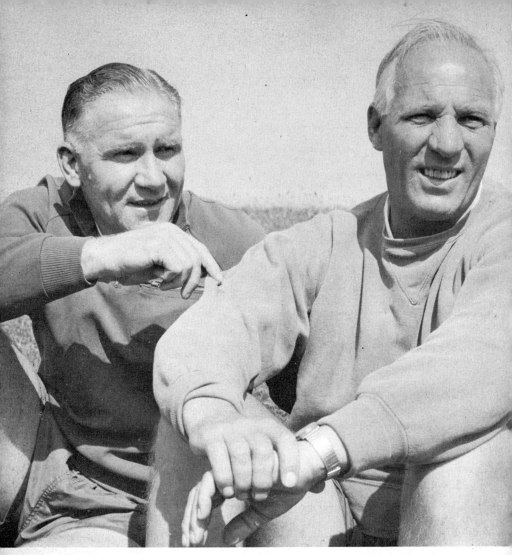

Here are the two men who must always be on the ball in as far as their jobs are concerned. They are the Spurs manager Bill Nicholson on the left and his assistant Eddie Baily.

and represented Middlesex and London. Cricket was as important to him in those days as Soccer and he nearly chose the summer game for a career. He played for Essex Club and Ground as a 15-year-old.

But a Hackney-Edmonton schoolboy match at the Barrass Stadium, Edmonton, changed those thoughts. Hackney lost 3–1 against a side including Sonny Walters and Jack Chisholm—but

13-year-old Eddie Baily was a stand-out in the losing side.

'I was a small little so-and-so in those days—I used to wear glasses,' recalls Eddie. 'I had a lazy eye'.

But, on the Monday evening following the Edmonton match, there was a knock on the door at the Baily house at Clapton and Jim Joyce, who is still on the Tottenham staff, announced, 'I am Dodger from Tottenham.'

The conversation went something like this:

'Dodger' Joyce—that's what he is nicknamed at White Hart Lane: 'You are Eddie Baily who played for Hackney Boys on Saturday, aren't you? I liked the way you played. Would you like to join my boys?'

Eddie agreed. 'To me it was a game of football,' he says.

That's how he first linked up with Spurs, and met the trainer of the time, George Hardy, a large sergeant-major type who, says Eddie, 'used to frighten me although he was a good trainer'.

Young Baily trained with Tottenham but, when he left school at the age of 14, he worked as a printer with the firm 100 yards away from his home where all his brothers worked. 'It was a ritual that we all went into print,' he says. 'I drew fourteen shillings as my first week's wages—and gave ten bob to my mother.'

Eddie is a product of the era of a maximum wage for soccer players—how much would he and his contemporaries be able to command today?—but finance was at the back of his mind as he played for Spurs Juniors for two years in the Wood Green League alongside Sonny Walters, another eventual member of the push-and-run side, Horace Woodward and Jack Chisholm.

At the age of 16 he was regarded as mature enough for further experience and he was sent to Finchley, the Athenian League side and a good standard amateur club. He changed his club—he changed his job. At the same time he began working in the City on the Stock Exchange.

Eddie got to Wembley Stadium with Finchley, who beat Southall 1-0 in the final of the Middlesex Red Cross Cup with a 40-yard winner from outside-left Freddie Boston, one of my own boyhood idols.

Wembley—the word spells glamour. Not for Eddie Baily and his Finchley colleagues at the time though. There was a 2,000 attendance to watch the midweek game that war-time day.

The next time Eddie returned to the famous stadium there was a full-house 100,000 crowd to watch England play against Ocwirk and the famous Austrian team of the day.

Eddie Baily's first game for Finchley was against Crossbrook Sports—and he collected a hat-trick in a 6–0 victory. Some debut for the 5ft. 6in. youngster who weighed a modest 9 stone 6 pounds most of his playing career.

He was still a Spurs amateur when he was called up for the Army at the age of $17\frac{1}{2}$, and service took him to Belgium, Holland and Germany as an infantryman.

'I was in the . . . Royal Scots of all things,' says Eddie. 'I reckon I was the only Cockney in the battalion, but it served me well later when I met up with Dave Mackay and Alan Gilzean. I spoke their language!'

Leave was hard to come by for a Serviceman at the time, but when the war ended Eddie was sent to play for the British Army of the Rhine side, a team of top professionals including the late Jimmy Cowan (Scotland), Stan Rickaby (W.B.A.). Billy Steel (Derby and Scotland), Eric Parsons (West Ham and later Chelsea), and George Lee (W.B.A.—now trainer at Norwich). The side stayed together as a unit and met visiting teams from home sent out to entertain the troops.

Eddie was the youngest member of the side and the only player who was unestablished. At that stage of his career he met Alex White, the Chelsea full-back, who asked if he played for a professional club at home. Eddie said 'no' and was advised to contact Billy Birrell, the then Chelsea manager, when he got back to England.

He did—and found that Alex White had written a letter of recommendation. Eddie signed amateur forms for Chelsea and trained alongside the greyhounds before leaving Stamford Bridge. Chelsea arranged to give him a game the following Saturday.

Fate stepped in and did Tottenham a good turn. The following Thursday Eddie was walking in High Road, Tottenham, when Jimmy Anderson, caretaker manager at White Hart Lane at the time, recognised him. He invited Eddie into the office for a chat.

'Want a game?' he asked, but Eddie told him he had signed for Chelsea.

'But you're amateur with us,' protested Anderson, brushing aside Baily's argument that he had been away for two and a half years and there had been no contact from the club.

'I'll straighten this out,' said Jimmy Anderson, and he telephoned Billy Birrell on the spot and persuaded him to cancel the forms Eddie had signed. What's more he signed Eddie as a professional at the same meeting.

Let Eddie tell it in his own words, 'In the morning I was a Chelsea player. In the afternoon I was back with Tottenham. Two clubs in one day—and Spurs gave me £10 for signing plus putting me on the wage bill. Ten pounds was a lot of money in those days and I reckoned I'd rather play for Spurs than anyone else.'

On his next leave Eddie made his professional debut for Tottenham in a Midweek League game against Aston Villa on 20 February 1946, as a member of this forward line: Albert Hall, George Skinner, Jimmy Jinks (Millwall), Baily, Charlie Whitchurch.

The goalkeeper was Bill Hughes, Ron Burgess was at left-half, Fred Hall (a guest player from Blackburn) at centre-half and Captain Roy White at right-half. Opposing Baily in the Villa side that day was Harry Parkes, now a director of the club. Another winning debut for Baily, though, Jinks scoring two goals in a 3–0 win.

Eddie played for the reserves when he was demobbed from the Army in November 1947, and the first game was a 4–1 success against Charlton. Joe Jobling, a famous Charlton name of the pre-war era, was opposing Baily, who had the ability to go by a player who was nearing the end of his career. 'Steady down a bit, son,' Jobling entreated.

Joe Hulme, who was managing Spurs at the time, called Eddie into the first team after four reserve appearances—and a career of some 380 senior games was under way.

Eddie Baily was a member of the side that reached new heights under Arthur Rowe, the fabulous push-and-run side that many consider the best team Tottenham has ever produced. How did it happen?

Eddie says, 'Basically, at the time we had a collection of players who realised that the simple things in soccer pay. It happens once every now and again.

'We were all basically good passers of the ball, and there was a box of talent in the side that was very, very good. Two fine wing-halves, a good goalkeeper and we were O.K. at inside-forward. It developed into a push-and-run game—that was what we liked to play. Arthur Rowe saw the players who could do it and the two things married.

'The more we played together the better it became, until we got too old together and Tottenham found you can't replace good players.

'Great players go. It's hard to put a great player in their place.'

Eddie Baily reckons that his side played some 'wonderful

football', a statement that will get no argument from me nor, I imagine, from anyone who saw them play. What a pity they did not have the chance to pit their skills against European clubs—but the competitions of today were a long way off in 1950–51.

The Spurs of that era did meet Continental opposition, and they did well against them. The Austrians were the top side in Europe at the time and, in the space of two years, Spurs played their crack side, F.C. Austria, who fielded several household names, four times; Spurs won two of these meetings and drew a third.

'We regarded ourselves as champions of England and they were the champions of Europe,' says Eddie.

One of the meetings was in Brussels, a match played in thick snow for charity. The winners were due to receive a Cup and, when the match finished all square, it was decided to toss a coin for the trophy.

As the coin landed on the snow Ron Burgess, the Tottenham Captain, bent down and picked it up. 'Our Cup,' he announced— and walked off with the trophy.

'We thought we deserved it because of the way we had played,' laughs Eddie.

That match in Brussels in March 1952, was billed as 'The Champions of England' v. 'The Champions of the Continent'. Spurs, who had won the League title the previous season, drew 2–2 after what Cecil Poynton, their old trainer, describes as one of the finest exhibitions of football he has seen in a lifetime of soccer—the sort of display that would fill grounds every week of every season.

It is odd that Poynton and Spurs manager Bill Nicholson both pick as the highlights of their soccer careers a display by Arthur Rowe's push-and-run side on their way to the Second Division championship.

'The first 45 minutes was as near perfection as you could get,' says Nicholson, who was in the team that day.

Poynton says, 'It was raining quite heavily at Filbert Street, but the first 45 minutes of that game, with us leading 2–0, provided the best exhibition I have ever seen.'

Newcastle director Stan Seymour, who was at the match watching Don Revie, then a Leicester inside-forward, enthused to the Spurs' officials afterwards, 'I have never seen anything like it. If you keep it up you'll win the First Division championship let alone the Second Division.' He was quite a prophet.

Les Medley, Eddie Baily's partner on Tottenham's left flank. Eddie says: 'We developed a tremendous understanding and could do things together without realising we were doing them.

Spurs certainly kept it up. As Cecil Poynton says of that side, 'Eddie Baily moved the ball faster and more accurately than anyone in a fast and accurate side.'

Now here, from the horse's mouth so to speak, is a player-by-player run down of that great push-and-run side—provided by Eddie Baily, one of the top cogs in the Arthur Rowe machine.

| | |
|---|---|
| *Ted Ditchburn:* | At that stage he was one of the three best goal-keepers in England. He was certainly the best club keeper, without being the best for the international side. He was a fantastic catcher of a ball in flight. |
| *Alf Ramsey:* | A good full-back—he could read a game. His main asset was his distribution. He was a great positional player. |
| *Arthur Willis* or *Charlie Withers:* | Both wholehearted, tenacious players. Both good tacklers—you've got to have their type in any side. |
| *Bill Nicholson:* | I reckon we had the best three half-backs in England. Bill didn't want to be beaten. How you get a player with his attitude I don't know. He never gave in. |
| *Harry Clarke:* | He always reckoned he shouldn't be in the side. He came to Spurs from Lovell's Athletic and he thought he was inferior to the rest of us. We thought him unbeatable, a useful bloke to have around when the heat was on. |
| *Ron Burgess:* | A great player. He did everything, he ran, he tackled and he had skill. He was a good Captain by example. |
| *Sonny Walters:* | A team player. The type who was so important to the pattern that if he wasn't there at any time you knew you had lost something. He invariably did everything right at the right time, including scoring goals. |
| *Les Bennett:* | Unpredictable. If anyone was going to hold the ball it was Les. He was a very good player, though, and could do things on his own. He could tantalise, yet he had flair. And he was always good at getting a vital goal. If we won 1–0 you could bet it was Les in the box getting the one that counted. |

| | |
|---|---|
| *Len Duquemin:* | A good old-fashioned centre-forward of those-days. He was willing to take a lot of stick for the team and work up the middle. The right type to have at centre-forward—he was able to stick the ball in the back of the net. |
| *Eddie Baily* and *Les Medley:* | We developed a tremendous understanding and could do things together without realising we were doing them. Les was the easiest bloke to play to—we were the last club pair to play for England. |

That's the analysis of Eddie Baily, 10 times an England international, of his push-and-run team-mates. Let's consider a few more testimonials. From their manager, Arthur Rowe, who worked on the old soccer adage 'Show me a half-back line and I will show you a team.' Rowe says, 'A first-rate half-back line. I rate Ron Burgess, Alf Ramsey and Eddie Baily as irreplaceable in that side.'

Bill Nicholson says, 'Ted Ditchburn was a great goalie. He was unlucky not to win more caps.'

Eddie Baily moved to Port Vale for six months in 1955–56, when the great side was breaking up, and later to Nottingham Forest. He helped Forest to promotion from the Second Division. One of his happiest memories there was helping to beat a Spurs side including Tommy Harmer, Johnny Brooks and John Gavin 4–3.

Eddie watched the 1960–61 Spurs 'double' side in a Boxing Day match against West Ham, and he says, 'On that day they were a fantastic team. If there was a team to compare with ours that team did that day.'

When he finished as a player at Nottingham, Eddie joined Leyton Orient. He had attended coaching courses because he liked being in charge of players and amongst them and felt he had the personality and ability to coach.

'I had enjoyed my football and I'd been reasonably successful. Now I wanted to coach,' he says.

Johnny Carey was the manager and he and Baily piloted Orient to the unprecedented heights of the First Division. It was Baily's first chance to try out his ideas, and I can vouch for the impression he made on the other side of the soccer fence.

Tottenham's 5–1 defeat of Orient after they had trained all week to do well against his old club was his biggest disappointment

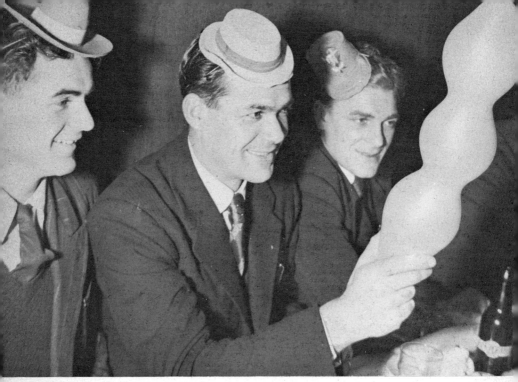

Len Duquemin (*centre*) and Sonny Walters (*right*) in party mood. They were consistent goalscorers in Tottenham's push-and-run championship side.

at Brisbane Road. He also recalls Spurs winning a Combination Cup Final, with Bobby Smith scoring the goal, before an 8,000 crowd.

In November 1963, Eddie was appointed coach and assistant manager of Tottenham—and that same night Spurs beat Birmingham 6–0. But the Tottenham team of the time was disintegrating.

'I knew what Arthur Rowe had gone through with our team of the 1950s,' says Eddie. 'It's the hardest thing in the world of football to keep a great team going. We have done reasonably well since then to have won the Cup and our reserve side have been champions for the past four years. Maintaining prestige is difficult, though. You can coach and advise all week. Your players still have to do it for you on the field. You are in their hands once the referee's whistle starts a game.'

Eddie says one essential a coach needs is to have his players working for him. A coach can only teach what he feels to be right.

'The pitch is the same now and there's still only one ball,' says Eddie. 'Football hasn't changed as a game. You still have to be a good passer in this game and as always you need skill. I believe in passing, but so many players today make this part of the game hard.

'There are only a few great and intelligent players today who can pass positively, the ball that beats a defender and creates a goal. There aren't enough creative players. As there are more defenders used in the game now you have to be a better passer than ever, even more accurate.'

For a skilled inside-forward that is, I'm afraid, a dying breed, Eddie bemoans the fact that football today is easy to destroy. It is easy, he points out, to tell players not to go into the opposition half of the field. 'There's no game and we might as well all go home if that happens,' is his apt summing-up of that defensive tactic. 'The game is only played because one player of a team runs at an opponent.'

He has always tried to teach players:
1. Be a passer and to be positive in all tactical situations.
2. To develop the attitude to want to play.

It is easy in soccer to go through the motions, easier now than when clubs had 40 professionals on their books fighting for places, and Baily reckons you have to coach the attitude where a player goes on the field saying I have *got* to get the ball into the net rather than that I will *try* and get it in.

As a product of an era of a 14s. first pay-packet and a £20-a-week maximum wage for players Eddie Baily senses the changes that unrestricted wages have brought.

'Football teams today should be younger,' he says, explaining that a player of 25 or 27 today who has been on top wages through-out his career has started to reach the running-down stage where incentive disappears. If a player survives that in the late 1960s he is really dedicated to the game.

Eddie believes that if a club has a team of 25 year olds who have played together with any success for four or five years that is the time to think in terms of rebuilding.

Spurs is a way of life to Eddie Baily. Even when he nearly went to Chelsea he was happy to rejoin Spurs—'that was always my club'.

The aim of all at Tottenham, he says, is to try and create the best team in the country every year. 'We try to get the players to keep us at the top,' says Eddie. 'It doesn't matter what we say or do it's the players who have to do it.'

Eddie accepts that the public (and directors and Press come to that) say that a coach is good if the team wins something, but he does not agree with the point. In football, he contends, there is a guarantee before the start of every season that 80 managers and coaches of League sides will not win anything. The players are the overall deciding factor of what a team wins.

His outstanding disappointment in soccer was not reaching Wembley with Spurs. Twice his side reached the semi-final stage to be beaten by Blackpool at Villa Park.

The first time they led 1–0 with four minutes to go—then lionhearted England international Stan Mortensen scored an equaliser and went on to complete a hat-trick in extra time. The second time Blackpool won 2–1, again after Spurs had scored the first goal.

'A Cup medal was the only honour I wanted,' recalls Eddie.

The best games he remembers were three 'fantastic' matches in 1950 when the push-and-run side beat Stoke 6–1, Portsmouth 5–1 and Newcastle 7–0 in successive home games. Of those 18 goals in three games, he says, 'We hit boiling point—and two of those games were played on mudheaps. No one could have stopped us then. We were devastating.'

He also recalls with a measure of pride his only League hat-trick in that game at White Hart Lane against Portsmouth. Spurs won 5–1, and Eddie dribbled the ball around the Pompey goal-keeper to score his third.

His personal 'bogeymen' in soccer were wing-halves, Jimmy Scoular (now the Cardiff manager), Alex Forbes of Arsenal, and Jack Snape of Coventry.

One player Eddie admired playing with was Wilf Mannion, the Middlesbrough and England inside-forward, who was six years his senior but 'a great player—my type of push-and-run player'.

Eddie has a 19-year-old son, Graham, a printer who plays as an amateur for Edmonton at the Barrass Stadium where his father was discovered playing years ago. Eddie and his wife, Elsie, also have a daughter, Jane, who is eight.

'I don't like gardening,' says Eddie, who lists as his hobby, 'sitting at home with my feet up on a Sunday and being miserable'.

Although I don't accept that he is miserable, he argues that he does not want to do anything but relax at home after the exertions of coaching all week and the ardours of guiding two teams on a Saturday.

Eddie has a hobby-horse about youth players. He is indignant with the school of thought that suggests that youngsters are wasting their time going to Spurs because there is little likelihood of

Arthur Rowe, pictured at home with his wife. He guided the Spurs side of 1951 to the League Championship.

advancement as the club buys ready-made stars. Every club buys players, even Manchester United, West Ham and Liverpool. Crystal Palace won promotion last season with 10 purchased players.

'It's a fallacy,' he says. 'If a player is good enough for Tottenham's high standards he will get through all right. We would like good youth players to come to us and get through. Youngsters will be given every chance.'

The Spurs' push-and-run side contained TWO players who cost a fee, Ramsey and moderately priced Clarke. Last season Spurs gave chances to several home-grown products to join the likes of Phil Beal and Joe Kinnear in the first team.

As Eddie Baily goes about his weekly routine his thoughts are on Tottenham of the present and the future.

But few of us who saw him play will forget the pleasure he gave in the past. He was an irreplaceable unit in a great side. A fine passer of the ball. A player who delighted in the simple and good things of soccer.

He first pulled on a Spurs shirt as a junior player and has contributed much to the club as a player and coach in the post-war years. He'll even be forgiven for thinking about joining Chelsea when he left the Army!

# Working Hobby

The local newspaper in Tottenham back in August 1943, carried a headline above the report of the 45th annual meeting of Spurs: 'Appointment of new directors causes a breeze.'

One of those directors was Fred Wale, today the chairman of the club and a man who has devoted years of his life to what he describes as a 'working hobby'.

The appointment of Mr. Wale may have caused a breeze—the reason was that the Board had seven directors instead of five—but the subsequent years have caused a considerable wind of change in the fortunes of the club.

When Fred Wale became a director in those wartime days of 1943 Spurs were 'in the red with the banks to the tune of over £40,000'. Today the club is acknowledged as one of the wealthiest in the land, a £1 million organisation that spends, for instance, £150,000 in one year on ground improvement projects alone.

Fred Wale, now 82, is the man at the helm of this modern-thinking organisation, a far cry from the Tottenham he supported in the first decade of this century when his favourites were 'Tiny' Joyce, Vivian Woodward and Joe Walton.

His memories of the club span the days from his early working career as an apprentice constructional engineer through to his retirement from business. He was managing director of a large engineering concern in Tottenham.

I asked Mr. Wale for his views on a director's function with a football club, what qualified a man for a seat on the Tottenham Board.

The first requisite he mentioned was a lengthy connection with the Tottenham club and district. Then . . . a director should have the time to spare for away travel.

'It is an insult for us to go away without a director to go into the home club's board room,' he said.

'A director is not called upon to pay for his travelling. He must look forward to it as a working hobby and give himself wholly to Spurs.'

These requirements are why, according to Mr. Wale, 'we cannot get a young man'.

Both the Tottenham chairman and his son, Sidney, who is the vice-chairman, keep a close check on the day-to-day running of Spurs. Chairman Wale is usually at White Hart Lane three times a week, excluding matches, and his son is almost as regular in his visits. .

The Tottenham ground is recognised in this country and abroad as one of the best in football. White Hart Lane is impressive, yet surprisingly compact.

It is a far cry from those wartime days when it was used as a rifle range and a site for the training of recruits in the evening. The corridors running under the stands were used for the repair of gas masks and a van set off most nights advertising for women workers to go to White Hart Lane.

Brick mortuaries were kept under the East Stand for those killed in local air raids and around the ground were dozens of pianos and other items of furniture stored after bombing raids.

Football stopped at the outbreak of war, but later Arsenal shared White Hart Lane with Spurs on alternative weeks when Highbury was bombed and taken over for Civil Defence purposes. Mr. Wale recalls 70,000 packed in at White Hart Lane to watch Tottenham play Q.P.R., and he remembers the day Spurs were playing West Ham when a 'doodlebug' cut out overhead and landed at Wood Green.

'A narrow squeak,' he says.

Willie Hall, Ralph Ward and George Ludford were three Spurs players who worked for Mr. Wale in the war—he gave Ludford time off to turn out as a guest for Millwall and earn a Cup winners' medal.

Ironically, Mr. Wale was born at Finsbury, which is Arsenal territory, but his one soccer allegiance has been to Tottenham. He became chairman in 1962, the year Spurs returned to Wembley for a second successive F.A. Cup victory. The following season

The close association between manager Bill Nicholson and chairman Fred Wale has been one of the pointers to Tottenham's success in recent years. On this occasion manager Nicholson receives a rose bowl to mark his 30 years with Tottenham.

they lifted the European Cup Winners' Cup—the first British side to win a major European trophy.

When Mr. Wale joined the Tottenham Board floodlights, let alone jet travel and European competition, were items of the future. Tottenham, in fact, with a £40,000 overdraft, were primarily concerned with getting out of the Second Division after the war.

'One of the first things I did as a director of the Club was to

use my knowledge from the engineering and building trades to help pull down this overdraft,' he recalls.

There were no evening matches then. Mr. Wale remembers Millwall supporters arriving at White Hart Lane for afternoon matches carrying their beer in one gallon jars.

So much for the past. It is the present and the future that concerns most of us now and the views of Mr. Wale on current trends was my main concern when I called on him at his home at Southgate.

Many supporters write to the Tottenham chairman saying: 'Why don't you buy so-and-so?' or 'You could get Bill Bloggs for £100,000 and he'd make a big difference to the team.'

The invariable reply from Mr. Wale to his correspondents, to those who sign their names that is, reads: 'Would you pay an extra ten shillings for your entrance money?'

Spurs, in fact, don't want to increase prices and the club directors are fully aware of the cost to an average supporter for getting to the ground, let alone for getting in.

There are hundreds of amateur critics . . . they pay their money and they are entitled to shout and air their opinions. But, mostly, they have no conception of what makes a club tick. Even a wealthy club like Tottenham has to keep a sharp eye on expenditure. Finance is a regular item on the agenda at the meetings of the Tottenham Board.

Fans take so much for granted and are apt to overlook the vast sums that are spent at football grounds for their comfort. In these days it is hard to maintain standards and impossible to make a song and dance about expenditure unless it is to boost the playing side of the concern.

Former club secretary, the late Reg Jarvis, receives the Football League long service medal. In this photograph chairman Fred Wale makes the presentation. *Left to right in the front row:* manager Nicholson, secretary Geoffrey Jones, the vice-chairman, Mr. Sidney Wale, Reg Jarvis, the chairman and director Mr. A. Richardson.

Nevertheless, it is a fact that Spurs spent £150,000 last season on the important, although unheralded, items of adding seating, altering seating, underground cables and additional toilets. Yes, £150,000.

Another project Mr. Wale and his co-directors have in mind for the south corner of the ground will cost £100,000. The floodlight pylons will be raised to give a better view and a further 600 seats will be installed.

When Fred Wale became a director of Tottenham, long planks in the West Stand were the standard form of seating.

Next time you moan about the performance of the team and reckon that the directors should dip into their pockets to provide the hundreds of thousands necessary to improve matters, stop and ponder the recent £150,000 that has been spent for the general comfort of all.

Spurs have always been to the forefront in supporting innovations in soccer. The club was one of the first to use pylons for floodlights—in the days when the pylons could only be 60 feet high and in reinforced concrete because of the problems of obtaining a licence for steel. The floodlights have been renewed several times . . . the lights and other innovations were provided with no fanfare of trumpets from the Tottenham Board.

Spurs have one of the finest training areas and a gymnasium under the West Stand that compares with the best. They have a ball court . . . the directors even provided a complete dressing room for the junior players with a reception room nearby for their parents.

'There is nothing we lack,' says Tottenham's clear-thinking chairman, who has plans for a ball court at the Paxton Road end of the ground on a factory site that the club is not going to let again.

## The Players

You can have the best appointed ground in the land, but it can be pointless unless a winning team is provided to play in the stadium.

Extra toilets are meaningless if you ignore the No. One item in a club—the playing staff. Tottenham's efforts in this direction have, of course, been well publicised, the 1960s have heralded the arrival of top international stars in a bid to keep the club at the top.

The chairman of a club is the man at the helm when it comes

The cockerel that stands proudly aloft White Hart Lane. Note the size in comparison with the local dignitaries of the time the cockerel went up.

to transfer fees. He has to sanction the expenditure of the vast sums needed in the modern transfer market.

'I accept responsibility for all the players we sign,' admits Mr. Wale. Manager Bill Nicholson attends all Board meetings, but the items of a player to be signed is not fully discussed at Board level in the early stages.

As Mr. Wale says: 'The buying of a player for Tottenham is discussed between the chairman and the manager. The close association between Bill Nicholson and myself has been one of the great pointers to the success of the club in recent years. I rely on his judgment when it comes to the players we buy.'

Mr. Wale, who sanctioned the deal that made Martin Chivers the highest priced player in soccer before Allan Clarke joined Leicester for £150,000, is interesting on the question of spiralling transfer fees.

'It could have been altered once,' he says, referring to the George Eastham case when the players might have accepted a raised maximum wage.

'The way these fees have gone up is bad for the game. You will find that all clubs today are looking to their reserve sides and youth movements to provide players.'

46

A benefit cheque for £750 and a special European Cup Winners' Cup medal for Dave Mackay—who missed the Rotterdam final. Members of the Cup-winning side watch as vice-chairman Sidney Wale (*left*) the chairman and manager Bill Nicholson acknowledge one of Spurs' all-time great players.

Spurs, of course, have splashed heavily in the transfer market in recent years. Last season they spent £100,000 on the virtually unestablished Roger Morgan. Did Mr. Wale's remarks indicate that the days of Spurs raiding the market to buy an established star were at an end.

'No,' he replied, 'but a player these days has to be worth £100,000 more than ever before. Clubs must draw a line somewhere.

'I THINK PEOPLE WOULD BE BARMY TO PAY £200,000 FOR A PLAYER—ABSOLUTE MADNESS.'

Mr. Wale believes that transfer fees should have reached their ceiling and he hopes that clubs will get together to make this a practical reality.

He went on: 'A player has got to be interested in football . . . as they used to be in the old days. I don't mind players being in business and safeguarding for their futures outside the game, but they should seek the advice of the directors of the club before setting out on a new venture involving their money and hopes.'

The Tottenham directors discuss outgoings at their regular meetings and know to a penny what they have available for new players or ground improvements.

47

Off to Canada and America last summer. Directors Mr. C. Cox and Mr. A. Richardson accompanied the party, pictured here as they boarded their plane at London Airport.

'From my point of view it is gratifying to know that we have still got 700 people waiting to go on to our season ticket lists—that despite the extra seats we have installed', he says.

The 'Glory, glory' may be somewhat muted as the 1960s draw to a close, but the Tottenham image still inspires 700 people to hope for a ticket.

The answer, I feel, is in the thinking of men like chairman Wale and manager Nicholson.

The Tottenham chairman told me: 'We must keep Spurs ahead. We must never go back.'

The Spurs manager admitted last season: 'You have to be successful or your supporters want to know why not.'

The Tottenham club, as a whole, works to the Nicholson maxim: 'We have got to be the best in the land, not the second best.'

It is this awareness of policy that keeps the average gate at White Hart Lane around the 40,000 mark. And why 700 people wait patiently for a seat. The fans feel that all that can be done is being done.

Mr. Wale looked at season 1968–69 when Tottenham finished sixth in the First Division table, reached the semi-finals of the Football League Cup and the sixth round of the F.A. Cup. Was it a bad season? Or bad by Spurs' own Everest—high standards?

'We were struck by injuries,' says the Tottenham chairman. 'We were looking forward to getting nearer the top, but our ambition is far from stifled. We want to get the Cup again . . . and the League.'

Spurs have never finished below eighth in a decade of manager Nicholson's reign, a fact that is overlooked in these days when runners-up are branded as failures. Sixth in the First Division could be construed as failure under those circumstances, but not by chairman Wale.

'Under the circumstances, with the injuries to Chivers and Kinnear, we had a successful season,' he told me. 'Not the sort of year we had expected, mind you but, from my point of view, satisfactory and a basis for the urge to do better next season.'

The partnership between chairman Wale and manager Nicholson was struck back in the late 1950s. Mr. Wale, then a director, offered the managerial post to Bill Nicholson, then assistant manager.

Mr. Wale recalls: 'I asked him if he wanted the job. He said "Rather". We have never discussed salary from that day to this, nor has he worked with a contract. There has been mutual trust and understanding.'

Mr. Wale sees Tottenham's future at White Hart Lane— 'Arsenal and Spurs have both turned down the Lea Valley project'—and it is interesting to know the thinking that has gone on to bring the ground up to super modern standards.

Spurs discussed the question of heating their stands SIX YEARS AGO. 'I tried it,' says Mr. Wale, 'but the cost is enormous. You need an enormous plant and, when you compare with what is required in a cinema, you can see it is out of the question.'

Spurs spent £10,000 on drainage at White Hart Lane last summer, and have ruled out thoughts of undersoil heating (as at Highbury) or all-weather pitches.

'We have lost only one match through ice,' says Mr. Wale. 'Undersoil heating is not the answer . . . the crowds who turn up prove that. Nor is false grass.'

Mr. Wale would like Tottenham to boast a larger car park area, but this is not possible because of the siting of the ground and, in any case: 'If our park held another 1,000 cars we would still be in trouble.'

White Hart Lane boasts new snack bars, a restaurant bar

49

that is 'as good as anything you could find in the West End' and a buffet bar. Present day catering problems preclude Tottenham going in for a luxury restaurant.

I asked Mr. Wale to name the highlight of his career as a director of one of the top clubs in the land, but he declined by saying: 'I have enjoyed every minute of my association with the club. At times it has been worrying and hard work, but my satisfaction has been the success of the club.'

Directors, strange as it may seem to those who envisage all soccer administrators as men with olde worlde thinking and archaic ideas on their relations with the players, have a human side.

Instance the Spurs decision to free Dave Mackay as a gesture of thanks to a fine club man when he said he did not want to finish his time at White Hart Lane in the reserves.

Mr. Wale and his co-directors decided to give Dave the chance to make some money by a move—'no other club would have done that', says Mr. Wale. There have been other examples of Tottenham's thinking on these lines in recent years, and Mr. Wale understates the case when he says: 'We have helped several players. We are always willing to help.

'The Tottenham club is closely associated with the private lives of our players.'

The Tottenham chairman has strong views on the minority hooligan element in soccer these days and also on the trend to defensive football.

'It is up to the magistrates to deal with hooligans,' he says. 'Not only to fine them but to give them imprisonment. Mind you, I think it will die down, but action is needed when a culprit is caught.'

On defensive football: 'You have got to look at every game as it is played, but I am not in favour of all-out defence. The crowds want attacking football and our aim, surely, is to entertain the customer.'

Who are the men who guide the fortunes of Tottenham? The executive directors are Mr. Wale and his son Sidney, a chartered accountant who is managing director of an engineering group of companies and a former Lieutenant in the R.N.V.R.

Mr. C. F. Cox, now retired from business, is a former Air Force officer whose father before him was a Tottenham director; Mr. A. Richardson is in the waste paper trade; newly elected Mr. H. G. S. Groves is a chartered surveyor with a business in Tottenham.

One of the many modern features at White Hart Lane. This automatic turnstile control enables officials to gauge the crowds as they enter the ground.

He is a member of Enfield Council and was a Lieutenant Colonel in the last war.

There are some 80 people on Spurs' weekly pay-roll. The club owns property and is a limited company. The fortnightly Board meetings embrace items as varied as £100,000 transfer fees to rents.

Being a director of a football club is no sinecure. Being a director of Tottenham carries with it the additional problems attendant with wealth and the responsibility of guiding a top club. The directors have sanctioned the expenditure of several hundreds of thousands of pounds in the past decade alone to make White Hart Lane into a more modern stadium.

Some people envisage a club director as a dignitary with the best seat in the ground to watch from and limitless free drink to consume after the match.

I trust this view is not too widely held around Tottenham. Fred Wale and his fellow directors have shown foresight and wisdom in helping Spurs to the pinnacle. Their aim is to keep the club at the top of the tree.

Even directors have to work at their hobby.

# Martin Chivers

Martin Chivers, the gentle giant whose transfer valuation was a mammoth £125,000 when he joined Spurs from Southampton in January 1968, was on top of the world when the blow fell.

He was carried off in the match against Nottingham Forest at White Hart Lane on Saturday, 21 September 1968, and missed the rest of the season.

Chivers, who I estimate cost Spurs £42 an ounce, scored on his début for Tottenham, but was only just settling down to peak form and to be appreciated by the White Hart Lane crowd when that knee ligament injury brought a premature halt.

'I was really enjoying myself at the start of last season,' Chivers told me last summer. 'The crowd were appreciating my play and I felt that they had accepted me just prior to the injury.'

The doctors told Chivers he had a 50–50 chance of recovery. Later there were more serious doubts about his ability to make a comeback. Southampton-born Chivers talks freely of the moments of anxiety and doubts, knowing full well that the dismal Jimmies said: 'He's finished—he'll never be the same again.'

Martin is a confident young man—he was 24 last 24 April—and his intention from the moment of injury was not only to come back but to come back as a star player in the £125,000 mould. There is a touch of Cassius Clay to the Chivers approach.

Listen to his words as he reviewed his all too brief Spurs playing career so far: 'I started off great, but then settled to an average game. I needed time to express my way of playing.

Martin Chivers—at 13 st. 4 lb. he cost Spurs approximately £42 an ounce.

Chivers in a mid-air tussle with David Webb of Chelsea.

'Most players with a big transfer fee on their heads take time to settle to a new club and to new surroundings and I was no different. But I was settling quite well when the injury happened in the Forest match.'

Chivers, who turned professional with Southampton and made his League début in the 1962–63 season, scored the winning goal for Spurs in his first outing for the club on Sheffield Wednesday's Hillsborough ground.

'It was a hell of a shot,' he recalls with pride. 'From all of 35 yards.'

Chivers scored ten goals in 23 League and Cup outings for Spurs to wind up season 1968–69, to add to the 13 in 24 games he played for Southampton prior to his transfer. A 20-goal-a-season man is worth his weight in transfer gold to any club.

And before the fateful afternoon against Forest, Chivers was

Martin Chivers speeding goalwards before his knee ligament injury
in September 1968.

well on the way to another 20-plus. He had scored six goals in 11
matches in the First Division and the Football League Cup.

'The fans were expecting something from me every time I
touched the ball,' Martin told me. 'I'd rather I had started badly
in my career at my new club—I've got a good few years at Tottenham left to prove my real ability.'

Although a comparative newcomer to the White Hart Lane
scene, Chivers is Tottenham-minded in his outlook. 'I can only
associate or compare with Southampton, my only other League
club,' he told me, 'and, in all honesty, Spurs is a different class.'

This despite the fact that the Saints had just completed their
best-ever season in the First Division and had jostled Spurs in the
top half of the table.

'They don't treat it as big business,' says Martin. 'Spurs look
after you in every respect, in little things like letting you sit in the

directors' box with the best seat in the ground rather than on the line when you are injured.'

Chivers is appreciative of all that Tottenham have done for him —and doubly appreciative of the faith and patience of manager Bill Nicholson, who gambled £80,000 and Frank Saul, one of the scorers when Spurs last got to Wembley, to bring the 6 ft. 1 in. marksman from the Dell.

'I don't suppose I could have been fit in half the time, but for Tottenham's urgency when I was injured,' he says. 'I had a police escort and was operated on in four hours. Tottenham arranged for me to have one of the top surgeons in England.'

A valuable piece of soccer property is Martin Chivers, all 13 stone 4 lb. of him. I remember calling to see him in hospital at Stanmore, Middlesex, the day after his operation and his first regrets at that early stage were for Bill Nicholson.

Martin told me from his hospital bed: 'He always had faith in me and I was just beginning to prove him right to pay £125,000.

'I FEEL MORE SORRY FOR HIM THAN I DO FOR MYSELF. He had backed me with his judgement and now I'm lying here. What's he going to do?'

What indeed? Part of the lack of success at White Hart Lane last season was obviously tied up with the missing link of Chivers up front in attack.

It is typical of Martin's sincerity that his thoughts were more for manager and club in the midst of his troubles than for himself.

At the time of his injury Chivers had played fewer than 30 games for Tottenham since his British record transfer—which was later exceeded by the £150,000 Leicester City paid to Fulham for Allan Clarke.

Joe Kinnear joined us at the bedside—Bill Nicholson had been an earlier visitor—and we were surprised at the cheerfulness and philosophy with which Chivers had taken his injury.

'I'm 23,' Martin said. 'That's a bit young to retire, isn't it? I'm told it's going to be six months, but I don't believe it.'

Well, it was all of six months. Chivers even missed the end-of-season tour to Canada and America last May, Bill Nicholson feeling it was too early to push him into competitive football of any sort. So Martin stayed behind for daily treatment and training for his eagerly awaited comeback.

Back to the hospital . . . we discussed the injury. 'It was all simple, a complete accident,' Martin told me. 'There was no physical contact with a Forest player, no pain when I went down.

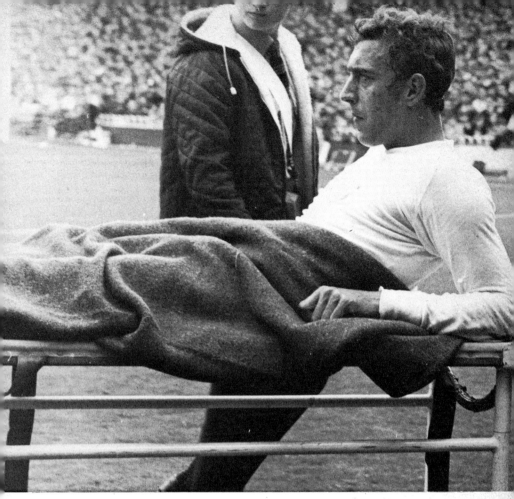

Martin Chivers is carried from the field after injuring a knee against
Nottingham Forest at White Hart Lane in September 1968. 'I had a
police escort and was operated on in four hours,' he says.

'My leg was numb and I couldn't bend it. Not until I woke up
this morning did I realise how serious it was.

'Bill Nicholson did not come down to see me after I was carried
off. He was really scared.

'I took a time to get through to the White Hart Lane crowd, but
all big money players go through this and only four of my 16 goals
for Spurs were scored at home.

'My wife broke down when she heard the news, but I have told
her it will be all right. Bill's the one I'm worrying about. He's a
smashing fellow and things were going his way again.'

I repeat the conversation because of the relevance it has even

57

months later as a pointer to the character of Martin Chivers. A player determined to repay the faith of a manager in him.

Martin spent two weeks in hospital, and most of last season on the build up of muscles in a bid to return to peak fitness. He was around the Spurs scene, a part of everything that went on, and refused to mope at his misfortune.

He relished the extra time he was able to spend getting to know his daughter, Andrea, and at home with his wife, Carol. Martin jokes: 'Apart from getting to know the family, I have been able to get on with some gardening. I'll be rivalling Jimmy Greaves before long.'

Chivers played for Southampton and Hampshire Boys before he became a professional player. He graduated to the England Under-23 side and played for Young England and the Football League.

Apart from being Britain's most expensive player when he signed for Spurs, Martin helped his new club to another record. His winning goal against Sheffield Wednesday in his first game for Spurs gave the club their first League win at Hillsborough for 30 years.

Daughter Andrea, too, was something of a record breaker as a baby. She more than doubled her birth weight of 8 lb. 6 oz. in three months at the start of 1968.

So that's Martin Chivers, the son of a father who played in goal for Southampton Boys and a German mother. A bright scholar at school—Martin collected five O-levels—who wrote to Southampton asking for a trial.

At The Dell he teamed up with Welsh international centre-forward Ron Davies, and the combination was feared the length and breadth of the land. Spurs hope that Martin can link with Jimmy Greaves and Alan Gilzean, like Davies a good header of the ball, for a similar goal-scooping combination.

These days Martin Chivers, his petite wife and their daughter live in a Georgian town house at Epping. He drives an expensive car.

His philosophy is: 'It's incredible that my old man works all his life in the docks while I get money for just kicking the ball about.'

Martin Chivers is the first signing Spurs have made from Southampton since Alf Ramsey joined them to become a vital cog in Arthur Rowe's push-and-run championship winning side. It is an odd fact that he is the most expensive player on the books, yet has still to attain international recognition.

The splashing of £125,000 on Martin Chivers proved that Bill

Chivers relaxing during a training session at Spurs' Cheshunt training ground. 'I need time to express my way of playing,' he says.

Chivers when he began training again last January. 'I'm 23,' he says. 'That's a bit young to retire isn't it?'

Martin Chivers jumps high to beat his former Southampton team mate, John McGrath, at White Hart Lane.

Alan Gilzean (*left*) who, Spurs hope, will eventually combine with
Chivers to provide a goal-scoring combination.

Nicholson plans to keep the emphasis on attack in his never-ending search for the successful blend for a new all-conquering Spurs.

The blow when Chivers fell out of the reckoning last season was a bitter one—but be sure of one thing. Martin has a mission in life. To repay his manager for his faith in signing him and the Tottenham club for all that has been done for him.

It is comforting to hear Martin say that he has years ahead of him at White Hart Lane. The fans had warmed to him by the time he dropped out of the side.

Bill Nicholson told me at the time that Chivers was showing the form he was bought for. I am sure that Martin Chivers, like Spurs, is aiming for the top.

To paraphrase Cassius Clay—he wants to be the greatest. In the greatest team.

# Mike England

Mike England, the gentle giant who earns general acceptance as the top centre-half in Britain, says of his first season as a Tottenham player: 'It went brilliantly.'

Mike signed for Spurs from Blackburn Rovers in August 1966, and that season helped the side to success in the F.A. Cup and near success in the League. 'We just missed the double,' recalls Mike.

Since 1966–67—nothing. Two seasons of disappointment. Spurs were summarily dismissed from the European Cup Winners' Cup by unfancied French side Olympique Lyonnaise in 1967–68 —Mike missed the two matches through injury—and were disappointing also-rans last season.

Injuries played their part in contributing to the comparative failures of 1968–69 and big Mike—he's 6 ft. 2 ins. tall—had his share of trouble. An ankle injury sustained in the 4–0 defeat by Manchester City at Maine Road on 12 October 1968, bothered him for the rest of the season.

'I carried it every week from that day in October until the end of the season,' says Mike.

Manipulative treatment was necessary and the doctors advised end-of-season rest in a bid to get the tall Welsh international ready for the start of a new campaign.

That's why Mike missed Tottenham's tour of Canada and America last May. He stayed at White Hart Lane for daily treatment before going home to North Wales for a well earned break

Mike England—generally accepted as the top centre-half in Britain.

Last season England had a spell as a centre-forward in the Tottenham
front line. Here Jimmy Greaves watches as big Mike outjumps a
Manchester City defender to head Spurs into a 1–0 lead at
White Hart Lane.

with his wife, Gwen, and two children, Darren, who is four, and Wayne, three.

Mike, who was born at Greenfield, near Holywell in North Wales, also used the time in the close season to move from his home at Cheshunt, near the club's training ground, to a four-bedroomed open plan house with double garages at Broxbourne.

Last season Mike played at centre-forward for Tottenham as well as centre-half, using his 13 stone 3 pounds frame and his renowned headwork up front as Spurs sought extra power.

'It's terrible playing when you are not really fit,' Mike told me. 'I played at centre-forward to help the side, but I must admit that I don't particularly like the role. The team was going through a bad patch at the time I was moved into attack—it wouldn't have been so bad if I was 20.'

He is, in fact, 26 and celebrates his birthday on 2 December. Mike is essentially a team man, which is emphasised by his view: 'I am getting paid to play anywhere, my wages aren't paid specifically for me to perform at centre-half, and I don't complain!'

It is little secret, though, that Mike prefers the centre-half berth, a position in which he has won some 30 caps for Wales at international level.

It may surprise a few fans, who see Mike as a massive centre-half pitting his skill against burly centre-forwards, to learn that he is a 'very shy' person, his own description.

'I am all right when I get to know people, but I still get embarrassed when I walk into a room crowded with people I don't know,' he says.

Listen to his summing up of season 1968–69 and you will see that Mike is very much a Tottenham man these days.

'I was hoping that last season would have been equal of my first with Spurs—brilliant,' he says. 'An average club would have been highly delighted with what we achieved, but Tottenham has had so much success it must count as a disappointing season.'

The crowd at Tottenham has accepted Mike England as a class player—he cost the club £95,000 when they signed him from Blackburn—but he admits that it took him a long time to adjust to life in the big city of London.

'I am accustomed to living down here now,' he told me. 'In fact, I have enjoyed the last six to 12 months. At first it was very difficult—coming from the North we didn't know any people and my wife took time to settle.'

Mike is 'very optimistic' about the future at Tottenham, par-

ticularly once he is 100 per cent fit and the other casualties such as Martin Chivers and Joe Kinnear return to peak form.

Things have changed for Mike in his three seasons with Tottenham and he acknowledges the debt that he and the side owe to Dave Mackay.

'I became accustomed to playing with good players when I made the move to Spurs,' he explains. 'It was great to play with Dave Mackay. I go further and say it was a privilege for me to have played with him.

'Dave was the greatest professional I have ever met. You can't replace a Dave Mackay.

'They will replace him, it is true, but there will never be another Dave Mackay.'

Mike's optimism about the future extends to the hope that he will win a League championship medal to add to the Cup winners' medal from 1967. And he has an unsatisfied urge to play in Europe.

'I only had two games in Europe with Spurs,' he says. 'I didn't play against Lyonnaise in 1967–68 because of cartilage trouble.'

His Tottenham highlights, he says, are confined to his first season with the club, not merely the Cup Final appearance against Chelsea but some of the wins of that campaign. 'I enjoyed that season—I just hope the next is as good,' he says.

Mike was an inside forward at school in Holywell, and after joining Blackburn as a 15-year-old ground-staff boy, he switched to outside right. Before settling at centre-half, he had a run at wing-half, and in his Blackburn days also had an extended run at centre-forward.

Listen to Johnny Carey, the man who brought England into League soccer 12 years ago. Carey, back with Rovers again after managing other clubs, says of Mike: 'He is the finest centre-half in the world. In my book no one can touch him.'

Johnny Carey always felt that England was destined for the top. 'When he came to Blackburn he was a thin, shy 15-year-old, but it was not difficult to see he would mature into a great defender,' he says.

Mike came to the notice of Rovers through a scout in North Wales, and manager Carey invited the youngster to Ewood Park for a look at his potential.

'His first matches for me at Blackburn were at inside-forward, but only because he was playing with boys much older than himself,' recalls Mr. Carey.

'It was obvious he would fill out.'

Mike England, the Gentle Giant, tackles Terry Cooper, of Leeds United, at White Hart Lane.

Blackburn drafted England, and two other now internationally-known names current England right-back Keith Newton and Birmingham marksman Fred Pickering, into the Blackburn youth team which won the F.A. Youth Cup by defeating West Ham in the 1959 Final.

Mike confesses to having a soft spot for Johnny Carey—'after all he was the man who gave me my first break.'

Manchester United, Johnny Carey's former club, looked favourites to sign Mike when the time came for him to move from Ewood Park. 'I thought I was going to Old Trafford, but United dropped out of the hunt,' says Mike. 'I was quite happy about joining United because it was in the north; Spurs were not in the reckoning in the negotiations at the time.'

Blackburn, I recall, wanted John Connelly, the England winger who eventually joined them, as part of the England deal. Anyway, Sir Matt Busby did not carry through and Spurs manager Bill Nicholson announced his interest.

England, who had wanted to leave Blackburn for nearly two years and had turned down a tempting re-signing-on fee bait, travelled south, met the Spurs players a day or two before the start of the 1966–67 season and signed to make his début against Leeds United on the opening day.

'What I saw of Tottenham was impressive,' recalls Mike.

August brings fresh hope to every football fan, but few White Hart Lane regulars could have envisaged, despite the advent of Mike England, the success that Dave Mackay and his men would enjoy in the 1966–67 season. A season that was to be climaxed with a quarter of a million jubilant fans jamming North London streets of Tottenham and Edmonton to honour the Cup-winning side, the new generation of 'Glory, glory' boys we felt.

The season opened with Spurs beating the strong Leeds side 3–1 at White Hart Lane, a good result and a chance for the fans to run their critical eyes over new signing England. Mike's début was unsensational—he was bothered by blistered feet!

Mike was concussed in the home match against Manchester United, the eventual champions, and the first half of that season was like his début—unsensational for Spurs.

Enter 1967, and the turn of the tide. From the 4–0 defeat of Newcastle United on New Year's Eve, Spurs gathered momentum. 'We went some 20 games without defeat and finished third in the League, missing the double by a narrow margin of points,' says Mike.

England is a Dave Mackay fan. 'Dave was the greatest professional I have ever met. You can't replace a Dave Mackay,' says England.

Spurs paid a record sum for a defender when they signed Mike England. His ambition led to his move; his skill helped Spurs tighten their defence and do so well that first season.

Mike's displays in the Cup that year, particularly in the semi-final against Nottingham Forest, were outstanding. He is acknowledged as one of the best headers in the game and he has improved all-round playing alongside Tottenham's other stars.

Yet for the first three or four months at White Hart Lane he says, he did not play as well as his Blackburn form or as well as he could. There was the problem of settling in with different players and also of living up to that £95,000 price tag.

Despite those teething troubles, England was still confident enough to announce before the third round Cup visit to Millwall, then unbeaten in 59 League matches at The Den. 'I have already made up my mind to shake hands with the Queen at the Final.'

Mike was there; the Queen was, in fact, represented by the Duke of Kent.

Like that other great Welsh centre-half of recent years, John Charles, Mike can justifiably lay claim to the title 'Gentle Giant'. He is as mild mannered and polite off the field as he is assertive and whole-hearted on.

No one benefited more from the arrival of England at Tottenham than goalkeeper Pat Jennings, who was grateful for Mike's command of the penalty area.

Mike has come a long way since he was in the same class forward line of a school at Holywell as fellow Welsh international Ron Davies. He has progressed to the top of the soccer tree, even allowing for the time off for cartilage operations and ankle bothers.

John Charles, that other Gentle Giant, was always his idol—Mike reckoned he was the greatest. But it was an Englishman on whom he tried to mould himself at the outset of his career, the former Stoke and England centre-half Neil Franklin.

I, for one, won't argue with Mike's assessment: 'He was a classy centre-half. He certainly impressed me.'

Jackie Charlton, the Leeds and England centre-half, is the modern player who wins approval from Mike, who has a quirk about mentioning 'bogey' players, the forwards who always give him a tough time.

'You certainly come across them,' he told me. 'There are certain players you hate to meet too often, but I just don't mention them. I know the feeling I get when I read a centre-forward rates me as the greatest or as his particular bogey-man—I feel great and go

I didn't like the taste of that, says Mike England as he chests the ball away after a high centre has beaten Pat Jennings.

out and play well against him. If I told the names of the players I don't like to meet it would give them the same superiority.'

A rational viewpoint, although Mike does stretch a point to name Johnny Byrne, the former West Ham and England centre-forward who left Fulham for South African football last summer, as a former tormentor.

'Byrne always gave me trouble,' confesses Mike. 'A clever player, always popping up on your blind side. I don't mind admitting my weakness against him now he's out of the country.'

Mike drives a 1300 Capri, confesses to being 'sports mad'. Golf and cricket are his particular favourites away from the soccer scene and he and Pat Jennings often link up for 18 holes. 'I used to play off seven,' says Mike.

The soccer scribes have dubbed him Mighty Mike. But it is not only in physique that he is larger than life. His thinking is expansive. He wants to live up to his rating as Britain's No. 1 centre-half; help Tottenham to succeed and get his chance of a real crack at European soccer.

He won't really be happy until Spurs are the premier side in the land and he can again review a season with those three words—it went brilliantly.

# Joe Kinnear

The two people who have had most influence on Joe Kinnear's career as a professional footballer with Tottenham are his mother Greta and former Spurs and Scotland half-back Dave Mackay.

Joe says his mother 'loves to play manager' and Dave just 'loves to play'.

'My Mum's a football fanatic,' confesses Joe. 'She knows everything about the game. She's as mad about football as I am.'

What about the great Mackay, who last season helped inspire and guide Derby County back to Division One?

'Dave and I have been friends ever since I joined the Tottenham club,' says Joe. 'I admire him both as a man and as a player, especially for his attitude to the game. He helped improve my football at White Hart Lane and has always been ready with advice.'

Mackay has twice broken the same leg while with Spurs. In January 1969, Kinnear broke his right leg in two places just above the ankle.

'We were playing Leeds at White Hart Lane,' recalls Joe. 'I was running for a long ball pushed inside me and rolling towards the goal line. Mike O'Grady, the England winger, was racing along on my blind side.

'At first I thought the ball would run over the line. But suddenly I realised O'Grady was moving past me and it looked as if he might just reach the ball.

'So I slid under him in an effort to flick the ball away. Just as I did, be brought his left leg back to cross the ball. His foot swung down and crashed into my right leg just above the ankle.

'I felt my ankle and although there was no mark on the skin, I remembered what Dave had said about his breaks and realised that the bone had gone.'

Joe was carried off immediately and X-rayed in the White Hart Lane treatment room. From that moment he began a six months' struggle to regain match fitness.

His leg was encased in plaster for the six weeks he spent in hospital and the six weeks immediately afterwards.

Once the plaster was removed he returned to training, jogging only at first and then building up to stamina sapping exercises on a stationary bicycle, and hours of running up and down the terracing at White Hart Lane.

'I had been told about the endless days Dave spent dragging his leg up and down the terraces,' says Joe. 'The physical effort required makes it hard work but I found it even more difficult adjusting myself mentally to the hours of training in isolation.

'In normal training we always have someone shouting and encouraging us. But throughout last summer I spent two hours in the morning and two in the afternoon running up and down the stands by myself.

'It was so boring that I could easily have become discouraged and fed up. But I knew I just had to keep at it if I was going to get fit.'

Joe's broken leg was the biggest set-back in his four years as a professional.

He was born in the Kimage district of Dublin and when he was seven the family moved to Watford. His mother was born in Dublin, but his father, Gerry, is an Ulsterman from Belfast. Watford is regarded as neutral territory!

Gerry Kinnear is a storekeeper for a Watford printing firm and concedes second place to Mum when it comes to soccer knowledge. Joe is their only son—the four other children are Amelia, 14, Louise, 15, Carmen, 24, and Shirley, 25.

As a schoolboy half-back, Joe captained his school, Watford Boys and Hertfordshire Boys, and supported Tottenham and Manchester United, but a career as a professional player was only a dream.

He left school at the age of 15 and took a five-year apprenticeship as a £6-a-week printer. How then, did he come to join Spurs ?

'I was playing left-half for St. Albans City, the Isthmian League

Joe Kinnear—'I won't accept defeat.'

amateurs,' explains Joe. 'Dick Walker, the Spurs talent scout, saw me playing one day and asked me along for a trial at Cheshunt.'

Joe played only the second half of this trial game but was one of three boys to be selected by Spurs manager Bill Nicholson. The other two were Steve Pitt and Jimmy Pearce, who both made the first team grade at Tottenham.

Joe signed for Spurs as an amateur in August 1963, and his youth team successes included helping his club win the Southern Junior Floodlight Cup. He was also in the side which beat Arsenal 1–0 in an International Youth Tournament final in Holland. 'Radford and Sammels were in that Arsenal team,' recalls Kinnear.

He signed professional forms for Spurs in February 1965, a few weeks after his 18th birthday, 'I was still in the print at the time,' says Joe.

'Bill called me into his office and asked how I would feel about turning in my job and signing professional. I wasn't too sure. It had taken me a long time to get into the printing industry. I had to go to night school after working hours and I thought I had a good future.

'But Bill persuaded me that my future was in football. So I signed as a £20 a week professional. I suppose I was lucky in joining the staff in this way because a lot of the youngsters who come to Spurs, do so when they are 15 and have to serve a two- or three-year apprenticeship.'

In April 1966 Joe made his League début against West Ham at White Hart Lane. 'It was a Good Friday,' says Joe, who is a practising Roman Catholic.

'I was over the moon about my selection for the first team, even though we lost 4–1. That day and the 1967 Cup Final were probably two of the happiest moments of my life.'

Phil Beal was the regular right-back until Joe made his League début. Joe filled the full-back position for the last seven matches, with Beal playing the last five matches of the season at left-half.

Spurs played four matches in Spain that summer. Joe was at right-back in three of the games and Phil played there in the fourth. 'It was touch and go who was going to start the 1966–67 season,' recalls Joe.

The fair-haired Beal played at right-back in the first three games of the new season, 1966–67, before he was moved to right-half so that Joe could regain his place at full-back.

Joe played eight first team games and then ruptured a thigh muscle in his right leg while training. Once again Phil Beal reverted to right-back. By now a keen but friendly rivalry had developed between these youngsters—the only two established players in that Spurs side who did not cost the club a fee.

Beal played 16 first team games while Kinnear was fighting to regain fitness. At the end of January 1967—four months after damaging his thigh—Joe was selected to play against Millwall at The Den in the F.A. Cup third round.

Millwall held Spurs to a goalless draw and Joe retained his place for the replay four days later. This time Spurs won 1–0, Alan Gilzean scoring the goal.

But Bill Nicholson brought back Beal for the next four games and it was not until 4 March that Joe was recalled. He played in the last 17 matches that season.

'Phil and I have always been good friends,' says Joe. 'And I was as upset as he was when he broke his arm, against Manchester City.' For that game at White Hart Lane on 25 February 1967, Joe was substitute.

Kinnear practising ball control at Tottenham's Cheshunt training ground. 'I'm poor with my left foot,' he says.

Joe Kinnear slides into a tackle with Eddie Gray of Leeds United at White Hart Lane in January 1969. Moments later Kinnear broke a leg.

'I was choked for Phil,' admits Joe. 'He missed the Cup Final against Chelsea in the May and although I was overwhelmed to be playing, deep down I think I was more upset for Phil.'

Joe was only 20 when he played at Wembley—the youngest player on the field. His mother didn't see the match. She was working at a fruit stall in Watford High Street.

Joe played brilliantly and helped Spurs beat Chelsea 2–1.

Kinnear played 35 of the first 36 first team games in season 1967–68, Beal coming in against Southampton.

Philip Beal was Tottenham's regular right-back until Kinnear made his League début against West Ham in April 1966.

Dave Mackay—'I admire him both as a man and as a player,' says Kinnear.

Joe admits he was playing badly when Bill Nicholson dropped him for a match against West Bromwich Albion in March 1968. Cyril Knowles moved to right-back and England Youth International Tony Want filled the left-back position.

'I was left out of the side to play Liverpool the following Saturday,' says Joe. 'I was particularly upset because it was an F.A. Cup game.'

Spurs drew 1–1 with Liverpool and lost the replay 2–1. And Joe was out for the rest of the season, apart from playing against Coventry and substituting for Knowles at Newcastle.

'It got to the stage when I didn't think I would get back in the team,' says Joe. 'That was the only time I thought of seeking an interview with Bill Nicholson regarding my future. Once you've played in the first team, reserve football does your game no good, especially if you are in the stiffs for more than a couple of games.'

Kinnear made his international début for the Republic of Ireland against Turkey in the European Nations Cup in February, 1967. A 30,000 crowd in Ankara watched Turkey win 2–1.

'I had gained seven caps at the time I broke my leg,' says Joe. 'But my major ambition is not in the international field. I would like to help Tottenham win the League Championship.

'I want to see them win the League by playing entertaining football. I admire teams like Leeds and Liverpool for their professional approach to the game, but I think Spurs can achieve the same ends in a more attractive way.

'It's good to win, and it's better still if you can couple winning with entertaining.'

Kinnear believes one of Spurs' troubles at the moment is that they lack a killer instinct. 'Dave Mackay had it, but I think he must have taken it with him to Derby.

'We're good to watch and we're professional, but some players accept defeat too readily. The Mackay attitude, the will to win, sometimes seems to be missing.

'Dave used to push his will into the players. He certainly pushed it into me and it has stuck. I won't accept defeat until the final whistle.'

Joe's chief worry other than his leg injury is his weight. 'I'm 5 ft. 8 in., and weigh around 11 st. I suppose that's about right. The lighter I am the easier I find it to play. When you face wingers like Ian Callaghan and Peter Thompson, it is essential that you can match their speed.'

As well as keeping his weight down, Joe practises constantly with his left foot. 'I'm not a two-footed player like Dave Mackay. I'm pretty good with my right foot, but poor with my left. So when I'm training I rely as much as I can on my left.'

Joe, who plays squash and tennis and enjoys listening to pop music, has travelled to the United States, Russia, Bermuda, Mexico, Spain, Turkey, Czechoslovakia, Poland, Holland and Germany.

'I'd like to do a lot more travelling,' he says. 'But my future rests very much with Cecil Poynton, the Spurs' trainer. He's terrific. If anyone gets me back into first team football, it will be Cecil. He's guided my comeback and what he doesn't know about legs isn't worth knowing! I certainly owe a lot to him.'

His mother, too, must take some of the credit for Joe's spirited fight to regain fitness. Each day when he returned home last summer after training on the terraces she was the first to ask 'How did it go?'

Mrs. Kinnear is a petite 5 ft. 6 in. blonde with a soft Irish voice, and a friendly nature.

'Joe was very inquisitive as a boy. I remember him looking up at me one day with his soulful eyes and asking "Mam, will I ever play for Eire?",' says Mrs. Kinnear, who bought Joe his first pair of football boots. 'I told him that one day he would.

'Naturally, I'm proud of him. I don't think people realise the years of hard work and dedication which go to make a professional footballer.

'I must admit, I am his severest critic. I don't go to the ground very often now but I watch all his televised matches.'

Joseph Patrick Kinnear, the modern day footballer who gets pop star treatment from his girl fans, is looking forward to another eight years in top line football.

As his mother puts it: 'The best is yet to come'—and she should know.

# Phil Beal

Fair-haired Phil Beal was first presented to a singularly unimpressed football public as a replacement in the Tottenham team for Danny Blanchflower.

The fans didn't quite scratch their heads and say, 'Phil, who?', but the news was the omission of Blanchflower rather than the promotion of Beal.

Next time out Phil Beal stepped in for Dave Mackay when the lion-hearted Scot was injured . . . and the Tottenham crowd waited for manager Bill Nicholson to make a big-money signing and for the home-grown product to fade into the obscurity of the reserves.

Well, it didn't happen like that. Stepping into the boots of a Blanchflower and a Mackay could have proved insurmountable obstacles, but Phil overcame the deputy tag and has emerged over the past two or three seasons as an acceptable personality in his own right. Which just goes to prove that a boy from the youth side *has a* chance at White Hart Lane to break into the big-time. Phil Beal may be a rarity as a product of the early 1960s—none of his contemporaries has made the grade at White Hart Lane—but, by golly, he proved it can be done.

In some 150 appearances for the Spurs, Phil has played in eight different positions. He has worn the 2, 3, 4, 5, 6, 8, 10 and 11 shirts as he has battled and given of his best for the club. A good chap to have around—and it is nice to feel that he has made a niche in the first team.

Phil is an unassuming 24-year-old who lives for soccer . . . and

Phil Beal – has emerged over the past two or three seasons as an acceptable personality in his own right.

Tottenham. Although he may not achieve the stardom of Blanch-flower or Mackay, his acceptance these days by a crowd used to big-money signings is reflected in his fan mail. Phil gets pestered by the autograph hunters and the seekers after photographs.

It was not always so. He was born at Godstone, Surrey, and played his early football for the Reigate and Redhill district side and then for Surrey.

A representative game at Charlton between Surrey and Kent brought him to the attention of Spurs' Harry Evans, the late assistant manager at White Hart Lane, who was impressed by the prowess of the eager left-half in the Surrey side.

Harry Evans wrote to Phil inviting him for a private trial, and the youngster jumped at the opportunity. 'I didn't know what I was going to do when I left school,' he recalls.

Phil signed amateur forms for Spurs in May 1960, and worked as an apprentice engineer at Oxted. He took time off for his three trials with Tottenham.

If the letter from Spurs had not arrived Phil could well be enjoying life today on the high seas. He had no ideas of a career and was so keen on life at sea that he wrote for particulars of a Merchant Navy job as a steward.

After his first trial for Tottenham, Harry Evans asked Phil if he would play for the juniors. He agreed, but wavered when his father felt that manager Bill Nicholson was not too sure of his making a success in football.

'Eventually Spurs asked me to sign and I dropped the Navy lark,' says Phil.

He played as an amateur in the youth side in the South East Counties League . . . well in the background as the famous Spurs 'double' side captured the imagination of the football public.

'No one else from that youth team has made it in the top flight,' says Phil. 'I must admit that I didn't think a great deal of my chances of getting through to the first team, but I was chuffed at being at Tottenham and part of football. That was good enough for me at the time.'

Spurs, it has often been said, had trouble getting good young-sters to White Hart Lane at that time because of the glitter of their first team squad and their willingness to pay money in the transfer market when top players became available.

Chances must have seemed limited at White Hart Lane. Phil Beal thought so . . . but he was still happy to be part of the club, albeit a quiet part.

John Sissons, West Ham winger, was in the England Youth side when
Phil Beal got his chance under Pat Welton, now on the Tottenham staff.

'I used to be very shy before I came to Tottenham,' he says. 'The office staff tell me how I have changed.'

Phil became a professional in January 1962, the season he gained youth international honours for England. He was called up for the England Youth squad at the age of 16, under the managership of Billy Wright, but had to take a back seat to prodigies such as West Ham's Martin Peters.

Pat Welton, now on the Tottenham staff, was the England Youth manager when Phil got his chance in the side a year later, alongside Ron Harris (Chelsea), John Sissons (West Ham), Len Badger and Bernard Shaw (Sheffield United) and Lew Chatterley (Aston Villa).

Spurs used Phil in their 'A' side and then the reserves but, although a professional from his 17th birthday, he had little to do with the big-name stars of the period. The late John White was very helpful to him though.

'I have seen a few comings and goings in my time,' says Phil. One of his contemporaries was Alan Dennis, the England school-boy international captain and left-back. 'I thought Alan was a cert to make the grade.'

Danny Blanchflower gave occasional encouragement to Phil and the other youngsters, who were in the care of Sid Tickeridge for youth team matches and Johnny Wallis for most of their training.

Manager Nicholson kept himself up to date with the prowess of the youngsters at evening matches, or at the Cheshunt training headquarters when the first team were not training because they had a home match under floodlights. Bill Nicholson used to take the youngsters for practice in the ball court at Tottenham in the afternoons.

Despite his youth international recognition, Phil was an unknown beyond the immediate confines of White Hart Lane when he was selected for his League debut in an away game with Aston Villa in September 1963. Beal for Blanchflower at right-half . . . and only because Spurs had two games that week and manager Nicholson wanted to save Danny for the second.

Manager Nicholson made a typically shrewd move before Beal's debut. He put Danny Blanchflower, who made the trip to Birmingham to see the match against his former club, in the same room as Phil. Danny talked to the youngster and offered sound advice. The text of his message was: 'Play your normal game.'

Phil did. Spurs won 4–2, and the ordeal of the debut was over. Bill Nicholson called on the youngster again, using him in a

88

midfield role as a wing-half, with Tony Marchi allying defensive duties with Maurice Norman. Then Spurs signed Alan Mullery from Fulham for £72,500 on transfer deadline day in March 1964.

'The first I knew about it was when I picked up the Sunday newspapers,' says Phil. 'I thought "that's the end of me".'

Far from it. Phil was soon switched to left-half and he adjusted his thinking. But he was far from established. 'I knew that if the right player came along Bill Nicholson would go for him,' he says.

The great Tottenham side of 1961 included eight internationals. No wonder Phil Beal did not feel too secure. It is ironic that the misfortune of one of the stars gave him the chance to make a positive mark in the senior team.

He was one of the four substitutes named on 18 November 1965, when Spurs played a Hungarian international eleven at White Hart Lane. That was the night Maurice Norman, a stalwart of the 'double' side, went for a 50–50 ball and broke his left leg in five places. Phil went on as substitute right-back—and has not looked back.

He had played two games in the reserves at right-back. And he stayed in the first team as a replacement for the unlucky Norman at Northampton the following Saturday.

Phil Beal (*centre*) and Alan Gilzean look on as Bobby Charlton (*not in picture*) beats Pat Jennings in a FA Cup match at Old Trafford.

Spurs had no recognised right-back and Beal's hopes were high. When Joe Kinnear missed four months of the 1966–67 season with a blood clot on a thigh, he seemed set to establish himself as the first choice No. 2.

But it was Beal's misfortune to miss the 1967 Cup Final against Chelsea . . . as a result of breaking an arm in two places on 25 February that year.

The injury seemed comparatively minor, but Phil was kept in plaster for a long, long time and did not play again that season. One nice touch was that Kinnear, who regained his place in the side and went to Wembley to gain a Cup Winners' medal, regularly visited his rival in his room at the hospital near White Hart Lane where he spent wearying weeks of inactivity.

News from the ground was the only thing that lifted Phil's spirits. He shared the delight of his pal, Kinnear, when Joe won his first cap for Eire and travelled to Turkey.

Phil was released from hospital in time to get to Wembley to see the Final—'I didn't enjoy it'—and to cheer Joe Kinnear in his place.

In season 1967–68 Phil went a step further to complete acceptance by the fans and played 35 games in the First Division, four in the F.A. Cup and two in the European Cup Winners' Cup.

The one-time deputy for Blanchflower, Mackay and, later, John Smith, was one of the major successes of the side in an overall disappointing season.

'I reckon I am a full-back now,' he has told me. 'At first I was just happy to be in the team, although I think I would have preferred one settled position.'

One of the highlights of last season for Tottenham supporters was seeing Phil Beal break new ground . . . as a scorer. His goal in the 3–2 defeat of Queen's Park Rangers at White Hart Lane was spectacular, as memorable to those of us who saw it as to the scorer.

'I picked up the ball just outside the Tottenham box,' says Phil, reliving the moment. 'I took it right through to the edge of the 18-yards line at the other end, squared the ball to Jimmy Greaves, collected a fine pass back from him and scored.'

That was the first time Phil had scored—and he had to run 80 yards to get his name on the sheet!

Phil and his wife, Valerie, have a baby son, Deiren—'my wife chose the name out of a book . . . it's Irish'.

In the summer he plays cricket for Godstone and has quite a reputation as a fast bowler. He tells me his major ambition in

90

Phil Beal (*foreground*) and Joe Kinnear (*right*), who replaced Phil in the 1967 Cup Final side.

sport is to get to Wembley to make up for his 1967 disappointment.

The worst day of his soccer career came in a Cup tie at Preston that Spurs lost 2–1. Frank Lee was the North End winger against Phil, the only time they have met, and Beal says: 'It was a nightmare. He turned me inside-out.'

He has far pleasanter memories of his trip to Malaga with Spurs in the summer of 1964 to play for the Costa del Sol Cup. His mission from manager Bill Nicholson: 'Shadow Eusebio.' The verdict: mission accomplished. Eusebio, one of the foremost players in the world, did not get a look in.

Spurs watched Eusebio scoring three goals for Benfica in a

previous match and questioned the marking of the Portuguese international. 'Go wherever he goes,' manager Nicholson instructed —and Phil obeyed.

'Eusebio didn't like it,' he recalls with a grin.

Spurs beat Benfica 2–1 and the headlines were for Beal rather than Eusebio, the sad-faced star who set the World Cup alight in England in 1966; the star who wrecked the North Koreans when they were three ahead—the power shooting ball artist the Wembley thousands voted a worthy personality successor to Pele in the World rankings.

Eusebio v. Phil Beal had the ring of trouble for the Spurs player. But it was Eusebio who finished second best.

I visited Phil in hospital when he broke his arm the following season and he told me: 'Eusebio is a great player, but he was not as difficult as I expected. He stayed put for me to mark.'

Eusebio stayed put! So did Phil Beal. The wing-half who was wanted by Q.P.R., Crystal Palace, Charlton and Aston Villa when he was a schoolboy began to make people sit up and take notice.

Rumour had it that Southampton wanted Phil as well as Frank Saul as part of the deal that brought Martin Chivers to White Hart Lane. I don't know if that is right—but I am sure that manager Bill Nicholson is glad he has Mister Reliable, in the form of Phil Beal, to choose from.

Phil does not come from a footballing background, but he has a cousin in Canada who married Czechoslovakia international Josef Jelinek . . . the same Jelinek who played outside-left for Dukla, of Prague, against Spurs in the quarter finals of the European Cup, in 1961–62. He scored the Dukla goal in their 4–1 defeat at White Hart Lane in the second leg.

That was when Phil was a youngster overcoming his shyness, with few thoughts that he would follow in such illustrious footsteps as Danny Blanchflower, Dave Mackay and Maurice Norman.

Phil did not envisage playing alongside players who cost Tottenham upwards of £70,000. It was a slow rise to recognition for him. But he has proved a point—that home-grown talent can flourish at White Hart Lane.

If the 'right player' becomes available now he will have a mature Phil Beal to contend with—still following Danny Blanchflower's advice and playing his normal game.

Still happy to be in the team.

# Jennings now Britain's best 'keeper

Ask a senior citizen on the Tottenham terraces to name the greatest goalkeeper in the history of the club and the odds are that there will be no hesitation in the reply: Ted Ditchburn.

Those of us brought up in soccer in recent decades would accept the nomination—until recently. For soft-spoken Pat Jennings, the 6-foot Northern Ireland international who is Tottenham's seventh post-war goalie, has emerged to test the Ditchburn legend.

I am not going to become involved in a Ditchburn v. Jennings controversy or analysis. Ditchburn, to my mind, is unquestionably one of the all-time great 'keepers—and I don't restrict my view to the confines of White Hart Lane.

But . . . there is no doubt in my mind that Pat Jennings is a top-rate successor to Ditchburn and, for my money, the best goalie in Britain at the moment.

I've heard the old hands at Tottenham watching rated 'keepers making fine saves and sneering, 'Ditchburn would have caught that one in his right hand.'

So has Pat Jennings. The memory of Ditchburn as the daddy of them all has lingered on through the 1960s to haunt all those who have followed in his stead.

Reg Drury, the top *News of the World* soccer writer, was weaned on Spurs in their Second Division days after the war and has always acknowledged Ditchburn as 'the greatest'.

Les Yates, the well-respected journalist who writes the Totten-

Jennings at full stretch, with Chelsea marksman Tommy Baldwin waiting in case there is a slip. Note how high Pat has jumped to crossbar level.

ham programme, has been a life-long follower of the club, and he admits, 'It is the generally held view that Ted was the best in Spurs history.'

Two sample views from men who have been around the Tottenham scene as observers for many years . . . and views that would find favour in all quarters.

But wait. Reg Drury, while pushing the claims of Ditchburn as 'the greatest of them all', also admits the qualities of the current man in possession when he says, 'At 24—and don't forget goal-keepers come late—Pat may become as good as Ted.'

As good, the equal of Ditchburn. Reg Drury says that Jennings could not better the old maestro, but he could become on a par with the all-time great.

Praise indeed, and, I think, deserved praise. Pat Jennings is certainly following in Ted Ditchburn's footsteps in one respect—he rarely misses a game.

Ditchburn made 247 consecutive appearances during his reign after the war. Jennings has missed only one League or Cup game

Jackie Charlton didn't reach that one—Pat Jennings punches clear from the lanky Leeds and England centre-half.

in the last three seasons.

Being an understudy to Ditchburn was a thankless task. So is being second string to Newry-born Jennings.

Spurs have fielded fewer goalkeepers during the post-war period than any other League club. The total is seven goalkeepers in 24 years—and two of them totalled three appearances between them.

This is the list: Ditchburn, Bill 'Archie' Hughes, Ron Reynolds, Johnny Hollowbread, Bill Brown, Jennings and Roy Brown. It's a fantastic record.

Hughes, who played for Newry, Pat Jennings' home-town club, before moving to Huddersfield and Tottenham, made two appearances in Second Division games, both of them against Nottingham Forest. He was transferred to Blackburn Rovers, with goalkeeper Stan Hayhurst joining the Spurs as part of the deal, and was chosen for Wales soon afterwards. Hayhurst was one of the 20 or so goalkeepers who have never got a look-in during the Ditchburn and subsequent eras.

Roy Brown, now with Third Division Reading, made his one first team appearance against Blackpool a couple of years ago, just after Scottish international Bill Brown was transferred to Northampton and Jennings sustained a rare injury and missed a match. Spurs lost 3–1 to Blackpool . . . Brown did not get another chance with the return of Jennings.

From Hughes, the understudy to Ditchburn who only got in twice, to Brown, the understudy to Jennings, who managed one game. Perhaps the unluckiest between them was Reynolds, who replaced Ditchburn at one stage but then lost his place to the White Hart Lane idol. Hollowbread was the eventual replacement when Ditchburn broke a finger in season 1958–59.

Seven goalkeepers . . . but only one name counted when Pat Jennings arrived on the White Hart Lane scene from Watford in June 1964.

'People were always on about Ditchburn,' Jennings recalls. 'Other players were always saying what a great goalkeeper he had been. People attached to the club kept on about it. I suppose Bill Brown had the same thing—it never bothered me too much.'

Jennings attributes the fact that it took him time to settle at Tottenham less on the fact that he had to live by comparison with Ted Ditchburn but more on the fact that manager Bill Nicholson was rebuilding the side at the time.

'There were so many new players that we made mistake after mistake,' says Jennings. 'It was my turn one minute, someone else's the next. Mind you, it was one heck of a step up for me from Third to First Division!'

Joining Spurs was altogether a step up for the shy young man from the Northern Ireland border town of Newry (population: 20,000)—a far cry from the days he was forbidden to play soccer at school and went to work in a factory.

Pat Jennings, now 24 (his birthday is 12 June), lives in a modern home in a quiet part of Cheshunt with his wife, Eleanor, a former show-band singer who comes from his home town. He drives a Jaguar car. He has adjusted to the life of a top soccer star in the big city.

Back home in Ireland Pat was the second of six brothers, the eldest of whom, Brian, is a winger with Coleraine and has been capped for Northern Ireland amateurs. There is also one sister.

'I was not allowed to play soccer in the school grounds at Newry,' Pat has told me. 'I had to play Gaelic football for the school, and, although I say it myself, I was about the best.'

Good enough, in fact, to be chosen to fill the 'midfield' position for the County Down Boys' team. But Pat also enjoyed his soccer and, at the tender age of 11, he played in goal in a local under-19 Youth League.

'I got a few buffetings from some of the older lads, but it never put me off being a goalkeeper,' he says.

Pat was lost to soccer for ten months when he left school. He went to work in a factory and had to work each Saturday. Finally he joined his father as a member of a timber gang felling trees in forests.

Newry United persuaded Pat to return to soccer at this time and he won an Irish Junior Cup medal with them at the age of 16. Newry were the best of 180 competing clubs in the competition.

Pat moved to Newry Town, still as an amateur, and there was talk of his being chosen for trials for the Northern Ireland youth team. In fact, he did not need a trial but was chosen on form—and left his native country for the first time to travel to Bognor as a member of the side contesting the 'Little World Cup' competition.

That youth tournament proved to be the turning point. Ireland reached the final and, although well beaten by England, the game gave young Jennings a chance to shine.

I well remember the impression Pat caused by his display in goal at Wembley in that 1963 final. Stan Barry, a well-known soccer scout who was with Watford at the time, travelled to Ireland in hot pursuit of the goalkeeping 'find' of the tournament. He knew that scouts from other clubs, some of them higher-grade clubs than Watford, had been watching Pat throughout the tournament and that the young goalkeeper had the chance to join any of the top Irish League clubs.

Playing in England, and at Wembley, had enabled Pat to extend the horizons of his thinking. The soccer bug had really gripped him and, as he says, 'I thought to myself—that's not a bad life.'

Pat says, 'I never thought we would beat England, but I felt we could have done better. Certainly injuries disrupted us.'

Who knows—if Ireland had done better, Pat Jennings might not have had the chance for a display of a lifetime that had the experts purring. Pat returned home to Ireland and a couple of days later Watford made their enquiry. Stan Berry arrived to sign him as a representative of the then Watford manager, Ron Burgess. Yes, Ron Burgess, the famous ex-Spur.

Watford beat off the opposition to the Jennings signature. 'I heard later that Jimmy Hill at Coventry was also interested, but

The one that got away—Pat Jennings, master penalty saver, cannot
stop this one from Chelsea's Peter Osgood.

he was under the impression that I was too small,' says Pat.

Too small? Watford paid £6,500 for the 16-year-old and it was a
gamble that paid handsome dividends.

'But for that youth tournament I could probably still be chop-
ping down trees,' says Pat. 'In Ireland it's only a chance in a
hundred that a League club will spot a young player.'

Odd, too, that the boy who was not allowed to play soccer at
school should make the top grade at the game, with due acknow-
ledgement to his experience in Gaelic football. Pat reckons that
playing midfield in the Gaelic game gave him confidence in
handling and agility, two of his outstanding assets as a 'keeper.

Pat replaced Dave Underwood as Watford's first choice goalkeeper and did not miss a match for the Third Division side—he
made over 50 appearances. Frank George, the former Leyton
Orient goalkeeper, was his unlucky understudy at the time.

Pat was holidaying in Ireland in 1964 when he received a
telegram from Bill McGarry, who succeeded Ron Burgess as
manager, calling him back to England for training.

Pat sensed that transfer talk rather than extra training might be
the reason for the urgency, but 'did not have a clue that Spurs were
interested'.

After negotiations stretching over a fortnight Bill Nicholson

He can't stop them all. A shot from Chelsea's £100,000 Birchenall (*not in the picture*) slides into the net.

travelled to Ireland to sign Jennings for Spurs for a fee of above £25,000. Pat won his first full cap for Ireland against Wales at Swansea in April 1964, and has since been an automatic selection for his country.

Although he was a full-blown, if new, international when he arrived at White Hart Lane, 18-year-old Pat did not settle with the bang that Spurs must have hoped for.

I reckon it took two years for him to settle, reveal his real top form and establish himself as No. 1 choice over Brown, the slim Scot Spurs had signed from Dundee. Perhaps Jennings was affected by his shyness.

He made his début in a friendly match in Holland against Feyenoord, the side Tottenham beat in the European Cup first round in 1961–62. Jennings conceded four goals in his début game —Spurs lost 4–3.

Cyril Knowles was another debutant for the opening League match of the 1964–65 season, and the two close-season signings played a big part in the 2–0 defeat of Sheffield United.

Reg Drury wrote of the new Tottenham goalkeeper, 'He showed Ditchburn-like qualities.' Jennings obviously did not keep it up, for Brown soon regained his place and the young Irishman was relegated to the reserves. That season he made 23 appearances in the first team, Brown 19. The following season Jennings got in 22 times to Brown's 20.

Although it took him two seasons to establish himself Jennings was obviously the 'goods' and he gained confidence in shouting for the ball and becoming master of his penalty area.

Let Pat put it in his own words, 'It was a big step for me coming to Tottenham. Looking back, I wasn't really ready to go straight in. It's experience you need in this game—and there's only one way to get experience, by playing. I didn't reckon I had established myself with the Tottenham crowd until I got into the side for good in place of Bill Brown. Then I started playing well.'

The goalkeeping aspiration for 12 stone 8 pounds Jennings has always been Gordon Banks, England's World Cup choice in 1966 and a regular member of Sir Alf Ramsey's squad, but also he expresses admiration for Chelsea's Peter Bonetti, another England international. He describes Banks in the simplest of terms as 'fantastic'.

Peter McParland, the famous Irish international forward, came from the same street in Newry and had an early influence on his life.

'Peter was everyone's idol back home,' says Pat. 'I never thought it could happen that I could emulate him.'

McParland, who began in the same youth league as Jennings, won a Cup Winners' medal in 1957 as a member of the Aston Villa side that beat Manchester United 2–1. Pat followed him on to the Wembley turf to collect a winners' medal ten years later, the day Spurs beat Chelsea 2–1 to take the Cup back to White Hart Lane for the third time in seven years.

Goalkeepers have their pet 'hates' among goalscoring forwards, the players who put an 'Indian sign' on them and give them nightmare experiences.

It is interesting to know that Pat Jennings concedes a team-mate as the forward he least likes to play against—Tottenham's own Jimmy Greaves. Even competing in practice games is enough to make Pat say, 'I don't like playing against Jimmy. I'd hate to meet him too often.'

Bobby Charlton is another hard-shooting marksman who earns a Jennings accolade—'he hits good goals'—and Pat has a weekly reminder on television of one of the Manchester United star's best. 'The Big Match' on independent television each Sunday in the London Area previews the programme with some fine goals, climaxed by one scored by Bobby against Spurs at White Hart

Lane. 'How about that?' asks the commentator as Charlton weekly bangs the ball past the diving Jennings.

How about that indeed? Pat needs few reminders of Charlton's shooting prowess, nor indeed of the skills of Bobby's Manchester United team-mate and his own Northern Ireland colleague, George Best, the 1968 Footballer of the Year.

'I'd rather play with Best than against him,' he admits. 'I suppose Denis Law, too, is another player I'd sooner not face too often. He's deadly near goal.'

What was the blackest afternoon of the Jennings career as a goalkeeper? He names his performance in a pre-season match at Hampden Park against Glasgow Celtic, a 3–3 draw against the then European Cup holders, but he adds, 'There have been a few nightmares.'

Pat doesn't like playing at Hampden and recalls conceding some 'terrible' goals, goals he could have stopped at other times and on other grounds.

'It used to depress me when I had a bad game or gave away a soft goal,' he says. 'Eleanor always tries to comfort me by asking, "What about the goals the forwards missed?" but I never see it that way. I'm more professional these days. I forget it if I have a bad 'un, but it really hurts you underneath.

'At one point early in my Tottenham career the crowd bothered me. Every time I went for a ball there was a buzz of expectancy, as if I was going to do something wrong. Now it's either O.K. or I don't notice.'

Goalies have more blinders than stinkers and Pat recalls with relish two performances of hitting peak form, one for Ireland the other for Tottenham.

He stayed with Mike England, the Tottenham centre-half, when Ireland played Wales at Wrexham in season 1967–68. England, as a Welshman, had the satisfaction of a 2–0 victory; Jennings the memory of an outstanding match.

The other highlight was his performance at Elland Road when Spurs staged a fine rearguard action in season 1968–69 to hold championship-chasing Leeds to a 0–0 draw. 'It was one of those days when everything hits you and sticks,' he says.

In the case of Pat Jennings, I submit, there are a fair proportion of days in a season when the opposition hate the sight of him and everything 'sticks'.

The Spion Kop at Liverpool loves him. So do the Merseysiders who watch Everton. Pat always plays well at both grounds and

How about it ref? Mike England appeals on behalf of Pat Jennings
as he and Mick Jones of Leeds crash to the ground.

describes the Anfield crowd as 'super'.

Note the strong humour when he says, 'They're probably
all brothers of mine.'

The week after his 'nightmare' match against Celtic Pat was in
the news—as a goalscorer. He beat his opposite number, Alex
Stepney, with a length of the field clearance. Did Ted Ditchburn
ever score a goal? I pose the question tongue in cheek.

Pat has been lucky to escape injuries to tot up his long string of
unbroken appearances. He gets over knocks very quickly. After
each match he is sore, but he shrugs off the aches and regards them
as an occupational hazard.

Pat Jennings is as nervous as the rawest recruit to the game when
a big match approaches. He begins to brood an hour before kick-
off. 'Bill Nicholson always says he likes me nervous and keyed up,'
says Pat.

He rates manager Nicholson highly as a leader of men and a

coach and is grateful for the help the Tottenham boss has given him by providing special exercises to sharpen his reflexes.

Often all the Tottenham goalkeepers—that's Jennings and his patient understudies—report back to White Hart Lane or Cheshunt, the club's training area in Hertfordshire, for special sessions with assistant manager Eddie Baily to develop their craft.

Playing at Wembley for Spurs was the top spot in the Jennings career to date. At the time, he says, everything was running smoothly for Tottenham and the sense of achievement in reaching the Final was as good as playing against Chelsea.

He concedes a certain amount of luck against Bristol City in the fifth-round at White Hart Lane, a late Jimmy Greaves penalty clinching a 2–0 win after City had missed TWO penalties ten minutes from the end with the score 1–0.

The referee judged Pat to have moved when he saved the first spot kick; Chris Crowe hit the second shot wide. How about *that* then?

Jennings has an enviable record as a saver of penalties and he also gets nomination as the goalkeeper with the largest hands in the game—a distinction he does not like too much.

Pat certainly has large hands—'it's a family characteristic, one of my brothers has larger hands than me'—but the emphasis on their size and blown-up photographs in newspapers used to bother him. He was rarely amused when people came up and asked, 'Can I shake your hands, Pat?'

'Made me seem something of a freak,' he says.

Pat uses his hands a lot these days to grip golf clubs. The golfing bug has hit him badly in the past couple of years and, where he used to joke 'my handicap is my clubs', he now plays off 14 or 15 and takes it seriously. He often plays at Crews Hill with Mike England, Cyril Knowles or Alan Gilzean.

He is an avid watcher of boxing and football, and a keen admirer of Dean Martin and any pop music. His wife, who has cut seven discs for Decca, says of him, 'He's so relaxed it isn't true.'

Pat is still around the house at 9.45 a.m. each day, with Eleanor doing the worrying about his being at training on time. Despite this she says of him, 'Pat is easy to live with.'

They met in Newry when Eleanor sang with a showband, but these days she does little professional singing because she does not want to travel from her home. Most afternoons she helps Pat, who has no outside business interests, with his fan mail, second only to that collected by Jimmy Greaves at Tottenham.

Getting down to work! Pat Jennings in action.

He received few letters in his early days at White Hart Lane. The final acceptance of Pat by the crowd has swelled his correspondence—and he takes his responsibility seriously by answering each letter and providing photographs and autographs when asked for.

A family in Belfast wrote to Pat asking him to visit their seven-year-old son when he visited Ireland for an international. Pat could not get to the hospital to see the boy, who had leukaemia, but he wrote to him. The lad died, but his mother told Pat that he treasured the letters from his favourite player.

'Pat was very sad at the time when he learned about the boy,' says his wife.

There is one outstanding ambition for Pat Jennings in soccer—to help Spurs to a League championship title.

I hope he makes it and adds a championship medal to his growing collection of caps and the Cup Winners' medal from 1967.

There are few better examples of a professional player than Pat Jennings, gentle and soft-spoken off the field but commanding and brave when the action is hottest.

Even the diehards may not concede he is better than Ted Ditchburn, but it is an Everest-sized compliment around White Hart Lane to be admitted his equal.

Pat Jennings and Mike England show their appreciation at winning the Cup in 1967.

# Roger Morgan
## —The Complete Professional

I was not surprised when the telephone caller at my home late one evening last February confided: 'Roger Morgan will be signing for Spurs tomorrow.'

It was a secret shared by a few in the know at the Tottenham and Q.P.R. camps that the 22-year-old twin was a priority target for manager Bill Nicholson, who revealed last season that he had spent around £900,000, on buying stars in his first ten years as Boss of White Hart Lane.

Bill Nick's first big buy was Dave Mackay—the buy he still reckons as his best. He was lucky in signing Dave from Hearts, for a £28,000 fee that, by today's standards, was a bargain. Come to that it was a bargain at the time.

'Dave was the complete professional,' says Nicholson and, without offence intended to any subsequent signing, Roger Morgan included, I must agree with the Spurs manager's assessment of Mackay as his top buy.

Luck played a part in the signing. Nicholson offered Hearts a fee he was sure they would reject only because he was interested in Mel Charles, then with Swansea, at the same time. When Charles, the Welsh international brother of Big John Charles, the gentle giant who has become a soccer legend in his playing lifetime, told Nicholson he had real hankerings after Arsenal that settled the matter.

In Nicholson's own words: 'I moved for Mackay, got him and never regretted it.'

What the well-dressed footballer was wearing last year! Roger Morgan, Spurs' £100,000 signing from Q.P.R., wore gloves to combat the cold soon after joining the White Hart Lane staff.

Although transfer fees have spiralled to the extent that Martin Chivers is valued at over four times the value of Mackay—and Dave was a *complete* professional—Bill Nicholson has never feared splashing big money for quality players when they become available.

That is why I was not surprised to learn that Roger Morgan was due to sign for Spurs last February, or that Bill Nicholson had tempted Q.P.R. with a six-figure fee.

For, let's face it, young Roger is a quality player—with the best yet to come. A fearless winger, one of the old-fashioned school who likes beating his full-back on the touchline side, with the ability to switch his game to the needs of the team.

I well remember John Smith, the Leicester City secretary who was with Q.P.R. at the time, telling me a few years ago: 'We have got twin wingers at Loftus Road who are going to zoom right to the top.'

My introduction to Roger and his twin brother, Ian, was at a photographic session soon after this conversation to introduce the boys to a wider soccer public.

Roger, the elder by ten minutes, says: 'It is easy to tell us apart.' Well, I can, but it took time to learn their characteristics and mannerisms. I dread to think what old-time football supporters would have made of the Morgans in the days when players weren't numbered.

Recognition came to the Morgans, who attended Chingford Secondary School for Boys, when they played for the Walthamstow district schoolboys team. Freddie Wilkes, a teacher, had been to school with John Basstoe, then a Q.P.R. scout, and he pointed out the promise of the youngsters.

That's where John Smith, Alec Stock, then the Rangers' manager, Jimmy Andrews, the coach at the time, and Derek Healy, the youth team manager, came in. They followed up the recommendation and became regular watchers of the Walthamstow games.

Just look at this for a team. In goal for Walthamstow was Derek Bellotti, who is now with Gillingham. At wing-half was Mike Leach, the Q.P.R. inside-forward who has attracted big-money attention from top clubs. At outside-right, and the star of the side, was a young man named Dennis Bond, the same Dennis Bond whom Spurs signed from Watford for £25,000.

The Morgan twins formed the left-wing partnership, and another talented youngster named Dave Wenham was centre-forward. Unfortunately, he had to give up thoughts of professional soccer because of injury.

108

That talent-laden Walthamstow schoolboy side that reached the quarter-finals of the English Schools' Shield drew managers and scouts from professional clubs from all over—most of them enthusing about the displays of young Bond.

Derek Healy, who played such a large part in finding the young talent that helped Q.P.R. rise from the Third to First Divisions in successive seasons, with a Football League Cup victory thrown in for good measure, had other ideas.

He told me: 'Everyone was watching Bond, but I was quite taken with the others. We tried to persuade Bond as well to join us, but I was quite happy with those we signed.'

The Morgans, Leach and Bellotti moved to Loftus Road. As they had to play for their schools in the morning on Saturdays, the quartet made their initial appearances for Rangers alongside Tony Hazell, now a first-team regular at Loftus Road, in the side that played in the Harrow Youth League. Bellotti jostled Peter Springett for the goalkeeping berth.

The Morgans? 'They were confident as youngsters and have made themselves players,' says Healy, their first mentor on the professional soccer scene.

Let Roger Morgan take up the story: 'We decided to try our luck with Q.P.R. because it seemed logical that we stood more chance of a breakthrough to the first team with a side in the Third Division. I took my G.C.E. examinations at school, trained with Rangers a couple of times a week at first, then became an apprentice professional.'

Rangers signed the twins as professionals on their 17th birthday and, as John Smith forecast to me, both have zoomed to the top.

It is ironical, considering the £110,000 that Spurs paid for Roger Morgan last season, that they did not consider him a prospect as a boy. It was Ian Morgan who received a letter from Spurs asking him to go for a trial, but he was committed to go to Rangers with his brother, from whom he had never been parted until Bill Nicholson made the break early in 1969.

As boys the twins stood on the terraces and shouted for the Lilywhites. John White was one of Roger's idols—the other was the master marksman Jimmy Greaves, today his partner in Spurs' costly attack.

Ian was the first to make his League debut for Q.P.R., against Hull at Shepherd's Bush on September 20 1964. Roger followed his twin into the side a fortnight later for a match at Gillingham.

The Morgans, as the only twins in top soccer, are unique, but Roger confessed to me earlier this year: 'I modelled myself on George Best on the way up, in appearance and hair style and characteristics. You have to make yourself known in soccer.'

The 5 ft. 9 in. twin—they both weigh 11 stone incidentally—was encouraged in his football upbringing by one of his grandfathers, 'Sonny' Pearson, a Walthamstow Avenue amateur in his day.

'He wanted me to go to the Avenue,' recalls Roger, who had to make a decision early on in his career between cricket and football. Essex, Middlesex and Gloucestershire wanted the Morgans to become professionals—'Ian was the better cricketer, I was the better footballer at that stage,' says Roger—and the summer game had an attraction because the boys were reckoned too small for football at one stage of their school career.

Their father, Ernie Morgan, good at tennis, and their mother, Joan, a keen sportswoman, encouraged the twins in sport and, as Roger recalls, 'We couldn't help being athletic.'

The twins share the same tastes and thoughts. Roger married a hairdresser, Marilyn, on March 31 1968. Six months later Ian married Christine—also a hairdresser. The Roger Morgans live at Waltham Abbey, which is handy for Tottenham, and the Ian Morgans live at Hoddesdon.

Let Roger take up the story of his signing for Spurs: 'I knew about the move on the Thursday evening (he signed the following day). Les Allen (the Q.P.R. manager and former Tottenham inside-forward) telephoned me at home at around 6 p.m. to tell of Spurs' interest and he said that the clubs had agreed to terms.

'Les phoned me back, and a little later Bill Nicholson came on the phone and asked me if he could call round at my house. I told him I had friends in for the evening and we agreed to meet at White Hart Lane. I spent two and a half hours with him—and just before midnight it was settled.'

The first move by an excited Roger was to telephone his twin to break the news.

'It was right out of the blue,' he says. 'At that stage I couldn't see myself getting away from Rangers, so I was delighted when Bill Nicholson moved in for me and the club agreed to release me. Tottenham is local for me—and I couldn't envisage anything better.'

Although he had not asked for a transfer—Rangers, remember, were struggling at the foot of the First Division table at the time and had been managed in quick succession by Alec Stock, Bill

Spurs manager Bill Nicholson thought he had split the Morgan twins when he signed Roger from Q.P.R. They still look pretty close here— Roger's first game for Tottenham, against Rangers.

Dodgin and Tommy Docherty—Roger Morgan had rowed with officials following the decision to axe twin brother Ian from the team.

'I was convinced I would never get away,' says Roger.

His first impressions of Tottenham left him breathless and gasping: 'Terrific.'

After the homeliness of Loftus Road, he found White Hart Lane vast and he was full of praise for the amenities, an indoor gymnasium and the weight training.

'It was like moving to Buckingham Palace,' was his summing-up. 'The training is interesting and varied, and there are a good bunch of lads at the club.'

Roger was not knocking at Q.P.R. when he spoke with admiration of Tottenham's bigger treatment facilities and the indoor courts. It amazed him to be able to train around the inside of the stand.

Roger Morgan won, six England international caps at youth level, and was nominated as a reserve for the Under-23 side on one occasion. How did he react to the vast transfer fee?

'I decided that I mustn't let it worry me,' he told me. 'I don't think I'm worth that type of money, but I didn't decide to pay it so the problem is not mine.'

The money he gets as his levy on a six-figure deal is spread over his Tottenham contract, and Roger's only concession to a move to the 'big-time' of White Hart Lane was to invest in a new saloon car. He gave up a sports car—a decision greeted with approval by his wife.

The rest of his money will be banked, although he and Ian may open a sports goods shop if the opportunity arises.

As one who has known, and studied, the Morgans for several years I will back Bill Nicholson's judgement in choosing Roger as slightly the better all-round player of the two. Rangers started to pick up last season, in their F.A. Cup defeat at Aston Villa, when Roger and Ian moved into the middle in a 4–3–3 set-up.

'I enjoyed that role,' says Roger, 'but, if Bill Nicholson wants me to play as an orthodox winger, or in any role, I'll be happy to oblige.'

The separation of the twins caused headlines in the sporting Press for, as Roger told me, 'We always talked to each other and were able to analyse each other's performances. We worked as a team, even to picking up our own image, growing our hair long and so on.'

The newspapers, in reporting the signing by Spurs of Roger and the splitting (in a football sense) of the twins, were emphatic that Bill Nicholson's £110,000 splurge was a half-completed coup because he wanted BOTH players.

The fact is that Ian was mentioned during the negotiations but, I understand, Rangers were not interested in an exchange deal involving Ian.

The Morgans, inseparable since they were schoolboy stars— they even holiday together each year—have shown skill, speed and bravery. Even with one Morgan Bill Nicholson signed flair, a much sought-after quality in soccer in these days of team method. The fee paid was a record in Britain for a winger, a record cash amount by Spurs for a player and the transfer fee beat by £1 the £99,999 expenditure on Jimmy Greaves.

Although soccer gossip linked Ian with Spurs earlier last season when he asked for a transfer, it was Roger who attracted Bill Nicholson. Roger spent the early part of last season recovering from a cartilage operation and recapturing the form that stood out before a 100,000 crowd at Wembley when Rangers won the League Cup in 1967—Ian did not play that day—and was on-form at the time of the signing.

Nicholson explained his decision to sign Roger at the time: 'I know he is Cup-tied, and we are not going to win the League title this year. So this is a player I have bought for the future.'

Spurs follow a policy of going for players who are available— and Roger Morgan became available at the time.

One of the strangest features of the signing was that Ian accompanied his twin to White Hart Lane and, despite being the minor partner on the day, shared the publicity glare of television and Press cameras and probing questioners.

Another twist to the story was that Roger's debut for Spurs was against Q.P.R.—and Ian—and he provided the final pass for a controversial Jimmy Greaves equaliser in a 1–1 draw at Loftus Road. He scored the Tottenham goal in his home debut, a 1–1 draw against Wolves.

I met the Morgan twins at Loftus Road on the morning of the transfer. We lunched together, and I accompanied them to their parents' home for a cup of tea before the signing.

Listen to Ian Morgan on the subject of their soccer separation: 'No one who is not an identical twin can know how close two people can become. We have always been on the same side . . . we queued together all night to get tickets to watch Spurs in the double year and the season of the European Cup . . . when Roger got kicked or had his cartilage I felt the pain.'

The Morgans can sign each others' names at their bank, Ian, who had two bookings against his name when Roger left Rangers to join Spurs joked: 'He promised I could use his name the next time I was in trouble with the referee.'

I shall long remember the story of the day of the Roger Morgan transfer of how he went to see his bank manager to say he was depositing £5,000—and being told not to join Tottenham. The bank manager, it seems, is an Arsenal supporter and he wanted Roger at Highbury! I am glad to report that he accepted the Spurs money at his bank!

So, Bill Nicholson, the biggest of soccer's big spenders, added Roger Morgan to the galaxy of talent at White Hart Lane. Bill Nicl s courage in the transfer market has brought the club rich rewards in his reign, a golden decade of League championship success, three F.A. Cups wins and a European triumph in the Cup Winner's Cup.

*Look at the list of buys:*

| | | |
|---|---|---|
| DAVE MACKAY | Hearts | £28,000 |
| TONY MARCHI | Juventus | £30,000 |
| JOHN WHITE | Falkirk | £20,000 |
| BILL BROWN | Dundee | £18,000 |
| JIMMY GREAVES | Milan | £99,999 |
| LAURIE BROWN | Arsenal | £40,000 |
| ALAN MULLERY | Fulham | £72,500 |
| PAT JENNINGS | Watford | £25,000 |
| CYRIL KNOWLES | Middlesbrough | £45,000 |
| ALAN GILZEAN | Dundee | £72,000 |
| JIMMY ROBERTSON | St. Mirren | £25,000 |
| TERRY VENABLES | Chelsea | £80,000 |
| MIKE ENGLAND | Blackburn | £95,000 |
| DENNIS BOND | Watford | £25,000 |
| MARTIN CHIVERS | Southampton | £125,000 |
| PETER COLLINS | Chelmsford | £8,500 |
| ROGER MORGAN | Q.P.R. | £100,000 |

As I said, it was no surprise when Roger Morgan joined the list. Nicholson's judgement bears scrutiny—and Roger is a good investment. I think his bank manager will agree.

The twins: Ian behind brother Roger, Tottenham's £100,000 capture from Q.P.R. Manager Bill Nicholson was the first person to split the pair in soccer.

# Jimmy for England

The chant has echoed from the terraces at White Hart Lane every time Jimmy Greaves has scored a 'special' in recent months, a constant reminder to Sir Alf Ramsey, one of Tottenham's most distinguished former players, that there is a strong school of thought in favour of an international recall for this marksman extraordinary.

I am not going to get involved in any argument on the merits or demerits of the decision of Sir Alf, as England team manager and architect of the 1966 World Cup success, to shelve from international duty one of the most prolific goalscorers of this or any other era.

I confess I subscribe to the viewpoint, long held by Greaves, that one goal scored with one kick in 90 minutes football can erase the memory of a poor 89 minutes, but Sir Alf is the expert. Jimmy, for his part, provides the most effective ammunition for the Ramsey critics while he keeps putting the ball in the opposition net.

He has been doing that rather effectively for more than a decade. With Chelsea, Spurs and England. In only one season has he failed to top the 20-goals mark in the First Division—and, don't forget, all of Jimmy's goals have been scored in the top class of English soccer—and the exception, in season 1965–66, came because he had hepatitis. He netted a mere 15 goals that season—in 29 appearances.

J. P. Greaves—that's what it says on his business card—is a

sincere and honest adult person. He is also a realist. Which explains his approach to his axeing from the England team after winning 57 international caps.

'It seems I am one of the few not surprised,' he told me. 'I didn't think for a moment I would be chosen.'

We were speaking just after the news that Jimmy had been left out of Sir Alf Ramsey's squad for an international against Rumania in Bucharest late in 1968—when Greaves was top scorer in the First Division and the 'Jimmy for England' calls were at their height.

Jimmy stood in the forecourt at Tottenham before a match and told me: 'Don't shed any tears for me—I don't want anybody doing that. They are only wasting their sympathy. I am not sorry · —I reckon I have had a reasonable run after 57 games for England.'

It was obvious that Jimmy, like Johnny Haynes, the former England skipper before him, did not fit into Sir Alf's plans. Jimmy accepted the situation as it was, and was perky enough to add this comforting footnote to the conversation: 'My main concern is scoring goals for Spurs and keeping Bill Nicholson happy.'

Jimmy Greaves scored 44 goals in his 57 appearances for the full England side—at that time he had made Bill Nicholson happy over 300 times.

The circumstances of Jimmy's 'disappearance' from the England scene have never been revealed in their entirety. Sir Alf Ramsey, quite rightly, has remained discreet but Greaves gave some indication when he told Peter Lorenzo, of *The Sun*: 'I told Alf point-blank that I thought my days as a front-rank international player were over and that, instead of being on the fringe of things, it would be better for me to lower my sights and confine my attentions and ambitions to the job I thought I could still do at club level.'

So, it seems, Jimmy wrote himself off from the England scene. Let Jimmy elaborate on the theme: 'As with everybody in the England set-up I have always found Alf a very honest, straight-dealing guy. He may have a clear, firm idea of what he wants, but as an old player himself, he is very understanding about the problems and stresses that are put on players more and more these days.

'Because of this open relationship, I went to see him after England had beaten Spain 1–0 at Wembley in April, 1968. I was in the 22 for that match, but didn't play. It was the night, incidentally, I sat in the stands to see Bobby Charlton score the goal with which he drew level with me on the 44 mark as England's record scorer.

'I TOLD ALF I DIDN'T THINK I WOULD BE OF ANY REAL USE TO HIM AND THAT I WOULD PREFER THAT HE DIDN'T INCLUDE ME IN ANY MORE OF HIS SQUADS OR IN HIS PLANS FOR THE FUTURE.

'He said he appreciated my problems and understood my feelings. Obviously he couldn't guarantee me a regular place in the side any more than he could any other player. This is the way of football at any level, let alone at the top, and so that's the way we have left it.

'It all might seem a little strange now, but you have to understand my feelings at the time and the situation as it was then. I wasn't scoring goals—it took me 19 games to score the last three of my 300—I had been dropped by Spurs, and I was ready to face things on a more realistic basis.

'I had even thought about moving from Spurs, but when I went to see Nick (Spurs manager Bill Nicholson) he told me the club wouldn't let me go.

'I wasn't bitter or twisted about things. I simply wanted to accept the situation as it appeared and work out my future accordingly.

'It's all right now for the crowds to yell for me to play for England, but they weren't shouting at the time. And the Press, who have been climbing on the bandwagon for Sir Alf to recall me just lately, weren't making similar noises then.

'After Nick told me Spurs still wanted me, I visualised myself as a second scoring string to Martin Chivers. I thought if I could get 20 goals or so a season I would justify my place and settle down to club football alone.'

So, what of those 'Jimmy for England' chants? Are they in vain? Has Jimmy written himself off for good and all as an international player?

I am pleased to record his comment: 'Let's put it this way. I am as patriotic as the next guy. If Alf wanted me for any training sessions I would be there on the dot. I am not big-headed or daft enough not to want to play for my country.'

Maybe, who knows, Jimmy will keep banging in the goals, the chants will continue—and Sir Alf might heed the call.

Jimmy is a great non-conformist and a tremendous rationalist.

Jimmy's on target again! He and Dave Mackay (right) use the flanks to good effect the day Dennis Bond got married. The groom seems happy enough.

As he quenched his thirst after a gruelling morning's training session, he discussed with me the question of goal-grabbing.

'It has become harder to a degree, although it was easier during season 1968–69 than in the previous two or three,' he told me. 'Scoring has certainly become more difficult, but the goals have been going in for me.'

That's a modest understatement from the goalscorer most feared in modern-day football. Jimmy accepts that most players in the late 1960s are more professional in their outlook than ever before and that the majority of teams are more tactically minded. He is prepared to argue whether this cuts out natural ability but, as a player of skill and somewhat an individualist, he is not bitter about the trend.

He accepts the planning as part of the soccer scene and realises the need to combat by forethought. But, rather plaintively, he says: 'The emphasis is on prevention rather than achievement.'

Perish the thought of the Spurs of not so long ago by-passing their natural attacking ability to plan a goal-less draw away from home. That's the way it is though, even though Tottenham today boast expensive forwards like Martin Chivers (£125,000), Roger Morgan (£100,000), Greaves (£99,999), and Alan Gilzean (£72,000).

'Everyone is more aware of not losing,' sums up Jimmy Greaves. 'Ten, twenty or thirty years ago a team approached a match with the ambition to win. Nowadays the idea is more not to get beaten. That makes it harder to score goals.'

Teams have cut down on the number of forwards they use as attackers and, to those of us brought up on an orthodox 2–3–5 formation, the trend to 4–2–4, 4–3–3 or what have you, is a step in the wrong direction. As Jimmy points out: 'You can have 20 or more bodies in one penalty area at one time, and that's where it counts for a scorer. We are combating the odds.'

He accepts the fact that there is unlikely to be a change in the system in his soccer lifetime with the words: 'Things will get worse before they get better. I was fortunate, if that is the word, to witness this defensive trend when I went to Italy and, although it was worse there in those days even than it is here now, it is still the same trend.'

I was delighted to hear Jimmy say: 'I don't think we'll go the same way'—the Italian way where there are often more matches played than goals scored.

How has Jimmy adjusted to this defence-minded trend? Well, he always subscribed to the point of view that one goal in a game justified his existence no matter how he played. Not so much now.

'I realise I cannot always score, the law of averages is against me,' he says. 'So I console myself by realising how many goals I make. I am happier in my mind now after a match even if I don't score.'

We talked after last season's 3–2 home defeat of Queen's Park Rangers, a game that proved entertaining to the crowd because of the likelihood of goals at both ends of the field from start to finish but not so satisfying to the modern tactical purist.

Jimmy's immediate reaction to his performance was disappointment. Then he considered the match as a whole. The first Tottenham goal occurred when his shot came off goalkeeper Mike Kelly for David Jenkins to net. The second followed an 80-yards dash by

Phil Beal to score in spectacular style—with a quick interchange of passes with Greaves near the Q.P.R. penalty area.

So, on reflection, Jimmy adjusted his thinking to realise that his contribution had led to two of the three goals. 'You have to accept this,' he says. 'Anyone who scores twenty goals in a season these days is a valuable asset so, if I can get twenty or more when I am half written off, this will suit me. There won't be many above me in the scoring charts if I manage twenty.'

If? Let's pause for a minute to study the Greaves scoring record for Tottenham.

1961–62, 21 goals in 22 appearances
1962–63, 37 goals in 41 appearances
1963–64, 35 goals in 41 appearances
1964–65, 29 goals in 41 appearances
1965–66, 15 goals in 29 appearances
1966–67, 25 goals in 38 appearances
1967–68, 23 goals in 39 appearances

Spurs certainly missed the Greaves goal touch when that attack of hepatitis kept him on the sidelines in season 1965–66—the only time he has not achieved the 20-goal mark in his career—and brought him his biggest disappointment—missing the 1966 World Cup Final.

Last season (1968–69) he again topped the 20-goal mark and it was good to see, as he pointed out, that 'old favourites' such as Denis Law and Geoff Hurst joined him at the top of the charts, alongside such a highly-rated newcomer as Joe Royle, of Everton.

'Goals have become tighter since the World Cup so any player who can still score 'em is worth money on the transfer market,' says Jimmy.

That's why a Geoff Hurst is rated in the £200,000-plus class by West Ham—and Spurs supporters shuddered when Stoke City were linked with the goals idol of White Hart Lane a year or so ago.

One remarkable feature of the Greaves career is the way he has retained his popularity with fans throughout the years. You don't hear moans about Greaves when he hits a lean scoring spell.

His image is good. He is a family man who is able to divorce his private life from his public, the father of four children, Lynn, aged ten, Mitzi, seven, Danny, six, and Andrew, three.

Danny Blanchflower, the former Spurs skipper and one of the players Jimmy most admired on the soccer scene, was godfather to Daniel, although the boy was not named after the popular Irishman.

Jimmy and his wife discussed several names for their newly arrived son, and Danny Blanchflower swayed the issue towards the child being called Daniel. But, don't forget, Danny Blanchflower was christened Robert Dennis!

Goals . . . goals . . . goals. Jimmy has scored some of the best the game has seen in recent years. He has popped a few in from close range. He has even been known to head a few!

I have often asked him his favourite of all time, and he plumps for the first he scored for Spurs when he arrived back from Italy because that helped establish him as a White Hart Lane favourite.

'I just can't remember which gave me the most satisfaction,' smiles Jimmy. 'The goal against Blackpool when I joined Spurs set me up when everyone was looking hard and saying "Here's this fellow from Italy—how good is he?" '

Bill Nicholson paid £99,999 to A.C. Milan for the Greaves signature. He did not want Jimmy to be tagged as the first £100,000 player. I see the reasoning, but could argue that Jimmy Greaves IS in a class of his own.

What about that debut goal for Spurs? Jimmy scissor-kicked a Dave Mackay throw-in, flicked on by Terry Medwin, past the Blackpool goalkeeper. He made it a memorable opening for Tottenham by notching a hat-trick.

A decade of top soccer has provided Jimmy with highlights and disappointments galore. His World Cup omission depressed him, but no more than the Spurs defeat by Benfica, the Eagles of Lisbon, in the semi-finals of the European Cup in 1961–62 season.

'We were good enough to win the European Cup,' he says. 'To this day I am convinced that we were refereed out of it. Three goals disallowed in two ties—two of them were mine—was a hell of a blow, particularly as we lost the tie by the odd goal.'

Jimmy Greaves is not a soccer watcher and does not anticipate staying in the game when his playing career comes to an end. He is a vice-president of Brentwood Town, the ambitious Southern League club near his Essex home, and reckons that going to The Hive, their quaintly named ground, will satisfy his football urge.

'It's difficult to imagine that far ahead when one is so involved,' he adds.

His remaining soccer ambitions are simple: to maintain 20 goals a season in the top class and, if he can avoid injury, to have a crack at overtaking the 434 record set up by Arthur Rowley, the

Jimmy Greaves, in the days when he was an England regular. Sir Alf Ramsey, the former Spurs right-back who is now England team manager and architect of World Cup victory, shakes hands with Liverpool winger, Peter Thompson, with England skipper Bobby Moore in the background and Jimmy (right) smiling approvingly.

former Sheffield United team manager, with W.B.A., Fulham, Leicester and Shrewsbury.

'It's not so easy in the First Division,' admits Jimmy, who was 29 last February 20, 'but with a little bit of luck I could see Arthur's record go.'

I have asked Jimmy to nominate the defender he least liked playing against, his personal 'bogey-men' or the tough-guy wing-halves who set out to nullify his scoring genius and succeed. No joy.

Jimmy reckons that some of his hardest games have been against average or limited players—he finds it easier to play against the great names and the top international stars. They know his weaknesses, he knows theirs.

Or, in other words, 'There have been a lot of players who have shut me out—too many to remember.'

The forwards he admires? Well, Jimmy hasn't the physique of an all-American, so it seems reasonable that he should turn to big, powerful men who are good in the air—he nominates Geoff Hurst, Ron Davies, the Welsh international who plays for Southampton, and Roger Hunt, his old English rival.

Strong, quick players who can take a buffeting earn a Greaves accolade. So do the 'floaters' of football such as Martin Peters and Colin Bell. The player who strikes quickly from a midfield position. 'I wish we had one,' sighs Jimmy.

Considering that Jimmy lost his place in the England side to either Hunt or Hurst in the World Cup Final of 1966 it is fine to hear his fair thinking on the subject of his rivals.

Of Hunt he says: 'You can be called a —— by fans all your soccer life. History proves what you achieve in this game. Roger must have been a good player over the years, the record books prove it with his goals total. We say Dixie Dean was a good player, regardless of whether he would have lived in the game today, so Roger will be looked back on the same way.'

What of Greaves on goalscoring? His philosophy is simple—and correct. 'If I miss a goal I miss it. To look for excuses to the crowd or in your team is pointless. I have got to miss 'em to score 'em. It's my job. That's why I try not to show too much jubilation when I net. Of course, I'm emotional—we all are. It's a question of to what degree you show your emotion.'

One interesting point that Jimmy makes is that scoring has been harder in the top class over the past five years and his own personal tally has gone down accordingly by some ten goals—'and that's half a season's work.'

Jimmy is a great person for self-analysis. This is how he sees Jimmy Greaves, the footballer.

'Apart from scoring the odd good goal, I am a bitsy player. I've scored lots of bitsy goals, finishing off from close range. It's anticipation and being in the right place at the right time that does it. One thing I have learned about scoring—EVERYONE COUNTS, whether it is a 30-yarder or a dribbly one. It's the old, old story. When you read the papers the next day you will find that it counted in the records as a goal and they don't bother to describe it there.'

Some of Jimmy's goals have been classics. He is happiest when he is scoring. As he says: 'It is my job.'

Jimmy emerged as a personality marksman in an era of unrestricted wages and has started to establish himself for the day when

Jimmy Greaves, the well-turned-out businessman, attache case at the ready.

the goals supply finally dries up with a packing materials business on the Southend arterial road at Romford, Essex.

He emerged as a Dagenham schoolboy. He was a scoring prodigy at Chelsea. Jimmy Thompson, then scouting for the West London club, persuaded young Greaves to follow many other boys from the Essex and East London areas to Stamford Bridge. Thompson saw Greaves, then only 14, score five goals in a match.

He introduced Greaves to Ted Drake, then manager of Chelsea, with the words: 'Meet the champ.' His assessment was not far off the mark. I still remember Jimmy Thompson telling me years ago: 'They say lightning only strikes once. It struck for me the day I saw Jimmy Greaves.'

By the time Greaves signed professional forms for Chelsea in May, 1957, he had won seven England Youth caps, an England blazer for a youth tournament in Spain, a Middlesex county cap and medals for Chelsea's junior side's success in the South East Counties League and Cup.

Chelsea recognised his budding goals talent by presenting him with an illuminated address after he had scored 114 goals during the 1956–57 season.

On the opening day of the following season the young prodigy was put into the League side—against, ironically, Spurs. The venue: White Hart Lane. The score: 1–1. Chelsea's marksman? Yes, you've guessed—Greaves.

There was to be nothing new in that debut scoring feat. Greaves has scored in every first match in which he has played from Chelsea junior to his first Cup Final in Spurs' colours:—

Chelsea Juniors
Chelsea third team
Chelsea reserves
Chelsea League side
England Under–23
England
Milan
Spurs
Spurs Cup Final

That's the list. Goals are his trademark and the reason why he will make top coaches wince with this Greaves-eye view of soccer: 'It is a game with one system—the scoring of goals at one end and the saving of them at the other.'

126

Me and my shadow. Chelsea's Ron Harris, closing in on Jimmy
Greaves, is noted as one of the best close markers in the game.

Few players have been able to shackle Greaves consistently as
he has marched from success to success over the years. Nobby
Stiles, England's wing-half in the 1966 World Cup, and Chelsea
skipper Ron Harris, two of the top destructive wing-halves in the
game, have probably come nearest.

Blanchflower was a wing-half who had an influence on Jimmy's
career. Jimmy rated him in the Super Super-Spur bracket as a
player and reckons Danny could slot a through ball from 30 yards
with greater accuracy than any footballer he has known. Greaves
is a respecter of soccer skill and he nominated Blanchflower as
right-half in his best British XI, adding that he was 'lost' at
Tottenham for a time when his former skipper quit the game.

Jimmy reflects: 'When Danny went and Dave Mackay fractured
his leg and John White was so cruelly killed the heart was torn out
of the Tottenham side.'

Greaves signed for Tottenham on November 30, 1961. He broke the club scoring record two seasons later. For three seasons he headed the list of Division One scorers, which was a new record since the Football League was founded in 1888.

Over 300 of the total of 400–plus goals that Greaves has scored have been in the First Division, the hardest competition of its kind in the world.

I was present at White Hart Lane in March, 1968, when No. 300 went in, Jimmy collecting two of the Spurs total of five against Burnley that afternoon.

Martin Chivers sent the ball across and Jimmy firmly headed the elusive 300th—he had waited over a month for that one—before receiving an ovation from the crowd that lasted well over a minute.

Odd that Jimmy should celebrate a scoring landmark with a goal from his head because one of my favourite Greaves stories concerns a Chelsea-Birmingham game early in his career.

'I went up for the ball and hit the goalkeeper under the chin with my head,' recalls Jimmy. 'They carried him off. About ten minutes later I did the same thing with his replacement. I seem to have this tendency for heading players instead of the ball!'

Jimmy is Box Office. He says that soccer is a branch of show business and that he is an entertainer. That sums it up.

In an era of Method teams and defensive tactics—the fan who joked 'We play a 1–9–1 formation' wasn't too far off the mark with some teams—he still continues to hit the goalscoring jackpot.

'If I have a bad game I don't go home and take it out on my wife,' he once told me, with a broad grin on his face.

The Greaves contribution to the Spurs success story of the 1960s is considerable. The 'Jimmy for England' chants may become muted as time slips by, but I am prepared to wager a healthy sum that his reputation at White Hart Lane will not dim for a long while yet.